Peeling Away the Label

Paul Elliot Martin

Peeling Away the Label

Growing up with ADD

Paul Elliot Martin

Write My Wrongs Co, United States
www.writemywrongsediting.com

Acknowledgement

Reilly Ribeiro for designing such an awesome front cover.

Contents

Meet the Author & His Intentions

Allow me to introduce myself. My name is Paul Elliot Martin. I am thirty-four years old. I have an attention deficit disorder (ADD) learning disability, which was diagnosed when I was in kindergarten. Now, I have a couple of academic degrees such as a Bachelor of Arts in theatre and a Master of Arts in teaching. In addition, I am seeking a special education endorsement that will enable me to teach students with learning disabilities. I am excited at the fact that when I complete the endorsement, I will be able to use my knowledge and experiences to relate to and teach children in a similar situation to the one I was in when I was younger.

This book originally started as a way for me to lift myself up after a recent job loss. At that time, I was in a negative mental state. I felt like a failure, and therefore, was quite depressed. Since it was difficult for me to clearly express to my family how I was feeling, they recommended I see a therapist. They hoped that with therapy, I would become more comfortable sharing my bottled-up emotions. Thankfully, I followed their suggestion.

At our first session, my therapist asked me a lot of questions to get to know more about me. After I told her everything I had accomplished, I commented on how that didn't come easy for me because of all the obstacles I faced with my ADD. Simply by explaining my triumphs, I started to notice a change in my demeanor. It was as if I was starting to climb out of this hole that I'd dug. For the first time since I'd lost my job, I smiled.

When our session was nearly over, the therapist gave me an assignment to complete before our next meeting. She told me to write down all the times I had faced an obstacle brought on by my ADD and how I overcame it. At first, creating this list seemed overwhelming. I found it hard to remember all the way back to my childhood years. However, taking the time to write down my thoughts on how my learning disability has affected me, and how I overcame each of those struggles, was an amazingly uplifting experience.

Once I finished the list, I started to see myself in a more positive light. First, I recognized that I am stronger than I give myself credit for. No matter the size of the challenge that was put in front of me, I refused to give up- at least not without a fight. This discovery helped me find the will to change my self-imposed label of "failure" to that of "survivor."

Second, despite my ADD diagnosis, and all the negativity that label brought, I didn't allow it to drag me down. Although many people doubted me once they found out about my situation, I was still able to achieve great things. I earned a bachelor's degree in theatre, a master's degree in teaching, and am in pursuit of an endorsement in special education.

After reflecting on all my accomplishments, and how inspiring they are, I realized there are not many books available to the public about a learning disability, the struggles that come with it, how to overcome those struggles, and how to have an awesome life despite being labeled with a disability. Even fewer books in the genre are written from the perspective of someone who has that disability, went through the same exact hardships, and, with the right amount of persistence, had phenomenal triumphs. Enter, Paul Martin. I hope by sharing my personal stories along with victories and defeats, someone with a learning disability, or someone who knows another with a learning disability, can relate.

Has anyone ever made you feel like you can't achieve something because of a diagnosed disability? Do you or a loved one struggle in life due to a disability? Have you or anyone you know refused testing for a disability because of the negative stigma that comes from the label? If you answered yes to any of these questions, then this book is for you. Take comfort in knowing that you aren't the only person or family who has endured all the obstacles that accompany a disability. I hope to convince you not to allow a label to make you doubt yourself or your abilities. My goal is to help you overcome these challenges and find happiness and confidence in who you are.

Since my initial diagnosis of ADD in kindergarten, I have had my share of challenges. My ADD adversely affected my ability to do well in school. My difficulties with fine motor skills, spatial perception, communication, and social skills resulted in stress on my self-esteem. Thankfully, I have a loving and supportive family who were involved in every way possible. I also had teachers and specialists who wanted me to succeed. With all this love and support, as well as my own persistence and self-initiative, I learned to overcome the label of being disabled, and all the stigma that goes along with it. Due to my ability to figuratively stomp-out all the negativity, I've been able to live a successful life.

Look at me now- I found inspiration to write a book about how I prevented my ADD from negatively defining me, and to convince others to have a similar mentality. I plead to those with ADD and other learning disabilities, do not let it be a reason to say, "I can't do this" or "I can't do that." Instead, muster the motivation to work exceptionally hard to achieve your goals. I am living proof that it is possible. By sharing my stories, and what I've learned on the path to successfully overcoming my ADD learning disability, I hope you can benefit from both my mistakes and my victories.

Part One: Characteristics & Labels

B efore we can ultimately reach a level of acceptance for all, we must first have a basic understanding of the two terms that are used to differentiate one person from another: labels and characteristics. These two terms are sometimes mixed together, despite there being a difference. *Labels* are how others see you. A person can have more than one label that is bestowed upon them. Unfortunately, more often, at least one of these labels have a negative connotation. A *characteristic*, meanwhile, is a "distinguishing feature or quality" (www.dictionary.com, 2002). In other words, while a label is how others define you, a characteristic is a trait that helps separate one person from the next. Personally, I think a characteristic has a more positive impact on how one sees himself or herself.

For some reason, having a trait or characteristic that defines you, and you, alone, has become a bad thing. I wish I knew the reason. Why would we want to be exactly like the rest of the world? I say, embrace your uniqueness, and don't allow someone to flip the script and label you as weird because you are different from them. They are just someone who is most likely insecure and is trying to feel better by bringing somebody else down. Do not let them change how you feel about yourself and your personal characteristics.

Allow me to use a math analogy to show the importance of accepting another's method or perspective. As someone who has been in the classroom as a middle school mathematics teacher and as a substitute teacher, I cannot help but observe a disturbing pattern. In some classrooms, students demean their classmates for writing a math problem or solving it in a different way than they do. I find that to be unacceptable. There is no need to look down on another person's method if you both get the same answer. For example, if someone writes 3 X 4= 12 instead of 4 X 3 =12, they are told it's wrong. Something is wrong, alright. What is wrong is our collective "my way or the highway" approach. If we allow a student to be shamed like that, rather than praising their creativity and effort, we are doing a huge disservice to them. It decreases the chance they will be willing to participate in whole-class activities and discussions. Therefore, they may become less enthusiastic about education and life-long learning. I mean, who would blame them for thinking that way if all they got was humiliation, instead of an encouraging education?

I, on the other hand, believe guiding one to use their strengths to solve a problem is a better approach. Let's say a student is having difficulty with a division problem and is more proficient in using multiplication. Since they are related, I would use multiplication to help them more confidently master division. For example, by using a prompting method, I would show a student who is struggling with a math problem like 6 ÷ ?= 3 that they can switch the numbers around and turn it into a multiplication problem. I would ask the student, "Three times what number is six?" They would say, "Two." At that moment, a light bulb goes off, and the student gets it. As a result, they are filled with confidence at mastering a skill that they previously thought was impossible. By using this type of teaching method, I utilize a student's strengths to help them, instead of having them struggle and become frustrated. This strategy provides much better results.

The lesson we can learn from my experiences is this: we needn't label each other, but instead, appreciate everyone's unique characteristics and approaches. By doing that, we show that we are a society of welcoming people. I believe that is something we should strive to be.

Chapter 1: Overcoming the Labels

One major hurdle in being a more accepting society is eliminating some of the harmful labels we use. For example, those who seek in-person counseling or therapy are labeled *weak* for attempting to get help. Why would it ever be a bad thing to improve yourself? I believe, from personal experience, that if seeing a therapist can give a person the insight to overcome their obstacles, it makes them stronger, not weaker. It gives one strength to acknowledge they want help and are willing to listen to suggestions on how to improve their chances of attaining their life's potential. Why is it a bad thing to improve yourself? After all, it led me to write this book.

Instead of bringing people down, we should be a society that helps to lift people up and supports others in their time of need. I used to allow the critical opinion of others about seeking help from a therapist influence my own decisions. I allowed these perceptions of being weak outweigh the importance of striving to become well. Therefore, I delayed seeing a therapist for the fear of a negative label. For what? For others to inaccurately judge me? I allowed everyone but myself to get in my head and define me. Well, not anymore.

I have realized only one person should label me, and that's me. I learned this through an exercise that my therapist suggested. First, I looked at myself in the mirror and saw the person I am. Second, I closed my eyes and pictured myself as I think society sees me. Third, I opened my eyes and saw myself as I imagined others defined me. After seeing the two images, and not liking the second one, I decided to make some changes. I started to embrace how I see myself and to ignore the doubters who try to tell me who to be or that I should be embarrassed for being different.

After doing the exercise and undergoing some therapy, I felt so much better. It was like I woke up from a deep sleep. Today, I am proud of the many characteristics that make me Paul Elliot Martin, both positive and negative. I suggest you try to find that same pride in yourself. Don't allow the labels people place upon you for being different make you feel you do not matter. After all, they do not define you. You do!

Chapter 2: Negative Labels Create Bullies

Negative labels not only create a problem with how you see yourself, but they also affect how others treat you. A person who wishes to dominate and disrespect you is called a bully. Once a bully learns of your perceived disadvantages, you are a walking target, and they are ready to pounce. Trust me, I know from experience with my ADD learning disability.

There are three choices on how to navigate through a bully problem. The first choice is to fight back. I did that when I was a young boy. In second grade, I was being bullied all morning by a student in my class. At recess outside in the school yard, I reached my breaking point. I was playing with some friends until this bully approached us. Once he targeted not only me but my friends, something went off in my head and I punched him to the ground where I kicked him several times. Immediately, I was taken to the school principal and was suspended for violent behavior. The principal realized the other boy had started the fight, and I was acting in self-defense. She would have been willing to be lenient with me if only I hadn't kicked the bully while he was down. What I remember most about this event is when I was told to call home, I very bluntly told my dad, "He started it, but I finished it."

The second, and better choice, is to ignore them. The moment you let your guard down and show the bullying has unfavorably affected you, the bully has won. Take away their power by simply being the bigger person and letting their immaturity and insults roll off your back. Once a bully sees they have no effect on you, they will move on to their next perceived target.

Your third and best choice is to alert a superior or family member to the inappropriate treatment. However, this method comes with a price. If you depend on someone else to come to your rescue every time an obstacle comes your way, it will be harder to be "your own person," and maintain a sense of independence. Throughout my life, I had to find a balance between how often I depended on help from others and fixing the problem on my own. It is still something I struggle with- not just for myself, but for others. There are times when I'm in a classroom, and I witness a student being mistreated. When I diffuse the situation, I want to achieve two contradictory things. First, I want to protect the victim so they know there is someone they can rely on. Second, I want to teach the victim they must stick up for themselves in the future. How do you protect someone without taking away their independence, fostering a high sense of confidence and self-esteem when they are older? When you find out, let me know.

So, what is the best solution? I wish I had the answer. It is something I struggle with myself. When I am the victim, sometimes I ignore the mistreatment and "let it go." Other times, I fight back. And then there are times when I seek comfort and guidance from another.

The conclusion I have come up with is that there is no "one size fits all" way to overcome negative labels and bullying. What works for one person might not get the same result for another. Personally, I think it depends on the situation. Do what you think is right to peel away the negative label. There's no easy way to defend against bullies but know you're not alone.

Chapter 3: Labeled *Confident* vs. Labeled *Weird*

I n Chapter Two, I laid out a variety of ways to deal with a bully. But what about dealing with the negative label itself? Possibly the single most effective way is to change people's perception of you in a more positive way. You can combat the negative label of weird without throwing one single punch. Instead, the strongest weapon you have at your disposal is self-confidence. Once you show people the only person's opinion of you that matters is your own, things will change for the better. Eventually you will not be seen as *weird* anymore. Now, you'll be perceived as confident or *independent*.

While replacing a negative label with a more positive one can feel tremendous, I can assure you it will not happen overnight. Let me save you time and warn you not to look on Amazon.com for an instant fix, like a magical wand. No such magical wand exists that makes the transition I speak of occur rapidly. However, with the correct amount of patience and persistence, you can make it happen. I know all of this from personal experience. I had to display a high level of confidence despite all the hurtful things that bullies said to me.

It wasn't just that people were mean to me; they were also constantly selling me short. I cannot begin to tell you how many times I've had to display a high level of confidence despite how many people underrated my ability to succeed. Yet, I somehow found the strength not to allow any belittlement to make me feel inferior. Instead, I mustered the courage to follow two inspirational goals: to successfully reach my fullest potential, and to prove my doubters wrong.

One movie that helps illustrate the importance of not allowing yourself to be underestimated is the 2001 film, *The Curse of the Jade Scorpion*. I have seen this movie countless times. Woody Allen not only wrote and directed the film, but he is one of the main characters, C.W. Briggs. Briggs is a private investigator who isn't taken seriously by his coworkers because of his unconventional methods of solving crimes. At the end of the movie, when he finds the villain, the bad guy immediately says, "C.W. Briggs, I seem to have underestimated you." Briggs responds with, "Story of my life. Everybody underestimates me. They think I'm a push-over. It makes my work much easier." I often recall this scene when others misjudge me as weak, and it motivates me to succeed even more.

You can learn from people such as myself and the character of C.W. Briggs in *Curse of the Jade Scorpion*. Instead of letting someone push you around, find the courage to fight back in your own way. Motivating yourself and overcoming the negative perceptions people may have of you, will instill in you a feeling of confidence and self-worth. Then you can walk up to a bully, look them in the eye, and say something like, "Yes, you might think I'm 'weird,' but I am proud to be my own person and to define myself instead of letting you define me." You don't necessarily have to say it exactly like that, but I'm sure you get the point.

Who did I turn to for help boosting my confidence during troubling times? My family. I highly recommend to anyone who encounters bullying, tell someone. I had a wonderful set of parents and an incredible brother to depend on.

Mom (Iris) & Dad (James)

Brother (Josh)

The person you reach out to doesn't necessarily have to be related to you. They could be a friend, a counselor, a doctor, a neighbor, or anyone you can trust. Like the Joker (played by Jack Nicholson) said in one of my favorite movies from growing up, the 1989 *Batman*, "Who do you trust?" (Burton). Indeed, trust your loved ones to help and be on your side. Trust them to build you up and protect you, allowing you to "live to fight another day." They are there—you'd better believe it— you just have to let them know what's going on.

I would not have the confidence I have today without the love of my family, especially my parents and brother. They were always willing to listen, or sometimes to defend me against my bullies, and they reinforced the picture I had of myself, encouraging me to ignore the naysayers. By believing in myself, I was better equipped to reach my goals and to prove my doubters wrong. As a result, those who may have regarded me as weird started to change their view and see me in a more positive light. All because I found the courage to not let their opinions cloud how I saw myself. You can do the same.

Chapter 4: ADD Label

In these times, I believe one label that is overused is *ADD*. Some who may not actually have the illness use it as an excuse. They say, "I can't do that. I have ADD." I cannot begin to tell you how offensive that is to someone like me who was diagnosed with the disability at such a young age and who has had to overcome so many struggles because of it. In my opinion, those people need to stop using their "self-diagnosed ADD" as a reason to give up easily. I have never used my ADD learning disability as a crutch, or as an excuse to not try. Instead, I will work two or three times harder to achieve my intended goal.

We, as a society, need to stop this mentality of "just give me the answer." An example of this mentality is when a student is struggling in school with a math problem, and their instinct is to go right for a calculator to get the answer. When I was a teacher, I would require my math students to show their calculations. To encourage it, I explained to the students that if they showed their work, they would at least earn partial credit. By doing this, I would test not only how a student got the answer, but also the calculation process they used, even if there was an error in the process. It is more important to identify our mistakes and correct them for the future than to simply give a response without evidence or justification.

Part of the problem is that most people associate being diagnosed with ADD or any other learning disability as a negative. If you ask someone who might have an undiagnosed disability why they or their family choose not to go through the testing and evaluations, it's usually because they don't want to stigmatize themselves. For some reason, a disability diagnosis is seen as a sign of weakness. Even former president and billionaire Donald Trump demeaned those with disabilities. When he was president of the United States, rather than using this powerful position as a symbol of inspiration, he got on the stage at a campaign rally and mocked a disabled reporter! That was the moment I saw him in a truly negative light. He had done and said things prior to that despicable gesture that gave me pause about supporting him. But because I was raised to give people second chances, I was willing to give him the benefit of the doubt. However, mocking someone with a disability as he did was the last straw.

Do yourself a favor—don't let other people cause you to think any less of yourself. As Michelle Obama, wife of former president Barack Obama, once said, "When they go low, we go high" (2016). To anyone with a disability, or who knows someone with one, don't let the label or its negative connotations define your future. I implore you to consider those words: a disability does not define you, but your strength and courage do. Demonstrate those most admirable of traits by not allowing the misguided to pull you "low." Instead, rise "high" above.

Part Two: Difficulties Resulting from a Learning Disability

This part of my book is devoted to all the challenges I have encountered throughout my schooling, and other areas of life, due to my ADD diagnosis. To those of you who have also been diagnosed with ADD, I'm sure you can relate to some of these difficulties. Take comfort in the fact that you're not the first, nor the last, to receive extra considerations that level out the playing field. One of the tools that has proven effective in helping to create necessary accommodations for students with special needs is an IEP (Individualized Education Plan). For those not familiar with IEPs, they are essentially a collaboration of recommendations to help a student with a documented disability to reach their fullest academic potential. School professionals—teachers, social workers, speech therapists, and occupational therapists—as well as the parents or guardians of a student with special needs attend a meeting with the goal to create a plan for the student's academic success. Sometimes the designated student attends. I was able to use the strategies discussed in my meetings to my advantage. If it were not for the accommodations proposed and implemented, I wouldn't be the success I am today.

There will be obstacles, and there will be ways to overcome them. It will be an uphill battle, but it can be done. I did it! And you can too!

Chapter 1: Academic Difficulties

A major part of my life that has been affected by an ADD diagnosis is my schooling. Luckily, with the help and support of my family, teachers, doctors, and other educational specialists, I have been able to overcome so many obstacles, enabling me to become the success I am today. One reason is medication. Ever since I was young, I have taken a pill every morning to help enhance my concentration in school. The name of the medication has changed so often, I've lost track. Variations of the medication were Adderall, Concerta, and Ritalin.

One drawback of the medication was that it did not allow me to consume caffeine to help give me a "second wind". By its nature, my medication was considered a stimulant due to its ability to increase my concentration and brain-functioning. As I grew older, I had many conversations with my doctors. Every one of them told me to avoid drinking coffee and other beverages that are high in caffeine. Any of these drinks mixed with my medicine would have had a negative impact on my body. Therefore, I avoided beverages with caffeine. It wasn't easy to do when there were moments in my life when I could have benefited from a small dose of caffeine to overcome any level of exhaustion I was encountering. But whenever I considered buying a can of Coca-Cola, I remembered the advice I was given by my doctors.

No matter what the medication, there was one thing that never changed—the shaky hands. This side effect didn't occur every day, but it was always part of my life. When I was nervous or putting a lot of pressure on myself, the intensity and duration of the shaking would worsen.

I might not like to take the medication or enjoy the side effects it created, but even I cannot argue with the good results. Thanks to this remedy, and monitoring its effects, I have been able to achieve success in school, earning a master's degree in teaching.

Yet, even with all the medication in the world, I still struggled with taking tests. When I was rushed during a test, I got overly nervous and made mistakes. To help eliminate those nerves, one accommodation I received, starting in middle school, was extended time during testing. This accommodation, hands-down, was a life saver for me. Also, I could use my personal computer during exams to help remedy the illegibility of my handwriting. Having a computer to use made a big difference too.

However, with extended time and using a personal computer, I still struggled in high school when I was trying to apply for colleges. There was a huge discrepancy between my standardized ACT test scores and my everyday performance in school. I scored an 18 on my national ACT test, which was not particularly high. Meanwhile, I had a 3.8 GPA (grade point average) out of 4.0, which was remarkably high. Therefore, to gain acceptance into any given university, I had to write convincing essays to the admissions offices of the various colleges explaining the reason for the differences. I was obviously successful because I was accepted to and graduated from Eastern Illinois University (EIU) with a bachelor's degree in theatre.

A few years later, while I was attending Concordia University, Chicago, in pursuit of earning a master's degree in teaching, I hit another snag. I had trouble passing one of the required standardized tests to become a licensed teacher. Twice I had taken one particular test unsuccessfully. On one of those failed attempts, I missed passing by only one point! I was really down about it until I decided to do something. I got additional study materials and found a tutor. In addition, the day of the test, my parents wrote me a heartfelt and encouraging letter. That letter made me realize I was not alone; I had the support of a loving family who would help me, whether I passed or failed. That gave me the inspiration and confidence to pass the test on my third attempt. It certainly is true what they say: "The third time is the charm."

At first, the academic difficulties I faced as a result of my ADD were challenging. However, with determination, support, and the help of certain accommodations, I was able to succeed. For those of you with ADD, I know you have the ability to achieve great things, just like I did. Remember these three tips 1) accept accommodations 2) work hard 3) believe in yourself! Speaking of believing in yourself, there's a saying I made up to encourage myself, "Roll up your sleeves and believe!" Basically, it means—do the hard work and believe in yourself. Remember this in times of self-doubt and reach for the stars!

Chapter 2: Fine Motor Difficulties

A long with academic difficulties, another part of my life that has been affected by the diagnosis of ADD is my fine motor skills. I do not excel in activities that require someone to use their hands. One of the activities that I've always struggled with is drawing. I concede that I'm the furthest thing from an artist. My drawings are subpar at best. Just ask two of my best friends, Courtney and Lyndsey, who I often play board games with. I originally met Courtney and Lyndsey on the EIU campus. They still live in the central Illinois area. I see them a few times a year for events like game night and an annual event called Friendsgiving. These events, which Lyndsey and Courtney invited me to, began as an EIU reunion of sorts. Now, they are simply annual traditions at which I get to see great friends.

At these get-togethers, where we often play board games, my fine-motors difficulties are amplified, especially when we play Telestrations. The concept of Telestrations is similar to the childhood game of telephone. One person writes a word in a notebook. They pass that notebook to a second person who makes a drawing relating to that word. The notebook is passed to a third person who looks at the last person's drawing and writes what they see. This continues until the notebook has been passed around the table to all the participants. At the end, the first word written, and all the interpretations are revealed. Obviously, the person who would be at the biggest disadvantage during the game is the one who had to look at my drawing and write down what they thought I drew before passing it on to the next player.

Even though Telesrations is a game I struggle with, I still have fun playing it. I get to enjoy the company of some of my great friends, and everyone can get a good laugh by looking at my drawings. It does not bother me at all. Especially because I laugh at other people's sketches, too. The fact that I can laugh at myself while having fun playing games with this group of friends demonstrates how I have been able to accept and move beyond my learning disability.

Another fine motor skill that I struggle with is writing. If you think my drawing is bad, it pales in comparison to the legibility of my handwriting. Essentially, I don't hold a pen in a conventional way. I cannot begin to tell you how many people have asked me why I hold it the way I do. Every time, I explain that this is the way I learned, and to change it feels wrong. You think that would've been sufficient. But no. They still gave me the face of judgement until they saw that even with all the dirty looks, they passed in my direction, I wasn't going to change. Think about that for a minute. People have, either intentionally or unintentionally, labelled the way I hold a writing instrument as *weird*. Well, I refuse to identify with that label. The method of holding a pencil that I learned when I was young served me well for many years.

Eventually my method from early on in my schooling began to fail me. As I got older, the fatigue set in. I couldn't write as fast, and the faster I tried to write, the more ineligible the writing became. This was of concern to my teachers and my parents. When I was in fourth grade, at an IEP meeting with my parents, teachers, and specialists, we all debated this problem and what accommodation should be put in place to help me succeed academically. My parents came up with an idea that changed everything. Knowing how much better I was at using a computer, they asked if there was any way that I could do the assignments electronically. The teachers and specialists at the meeting were very receptive, and dialogue started that would make it easier for me to do schoolwork for the rest of my school career. Prior to using a computer, I had to explain to my teachers what I had written on the paper. By either having my own personal computer or by using one of the classroom computers, I was able to hand in work that was printed neatly, organized, and legible. In addition, through the use of the computer, I have become an excellent typist. This accommodation helped me to succeed throughout my schooling and is proof that I was able to defy the odds thanks to the love, support, flexibility, and encouragement from my family and school specialists.

One teacher who agreed with my parents about the computer, and thus, advocated my using one, was my fourth-grade teacher, Ms. Chrisman. She had observed how fast a typist I'd become and how the assignments I completed on the computer were much easier to read than those that were handwritten. Not only did Ms. Chrisman advocate for my use of a personal computer, but she also voiced her concerns over my difficulty to learn cursive writing due to my fine motor limitations. She came up with the idea of teaching me to write my name in cursive and allowing me to use the computer for all other writing. Her rationale was that with the current wide-spread use of the computer, the only thing that a person would need to write in cursive was their signature. Thanks to Ms. Chrisman, I was able to avoid the struggle and embarrassment of unsuccessfully learning cursive in front of my peers. Instead, I had a newfound confidence derived from turning in tidy assignments that demonstrated my actual intelligence!

At this time, I would like to thank you, Ms. Chrisman. Thanks to your advocacy and support, I was able to succeed academically. The suggestions you made were very influential in my overcoming the ADD label.

Yet another difficulty I encountered due to my fine motor limitations arose during my middle school years. At the time, it was common to use a scantron for writing responses to standardized multiple choice tests. It was difficult for me to color in the tiny bubbles on the scantron. Therefore, at one of my IEP meetings, it was recommended that I have an accommodation called "No Scantron." On a separate piece of paper, I wrote down my answers, and handed it into the teacher. They used my answers to fill in a scantron for me. Thankfully, this "No Scantron" accommodation saved me a lot of time and embarrassment.

I have also needed to overcome my fine motor difficulties when learning other basic skills like learning to tie my shoelaces or a necktie, wrapping presents, riding a bike, and putting a key on a keychain. To master these abilities, I learned alternative techniques to accomplish the same goal. Through repetition of these techniques, I was able to get better at these tasks. By having a sense of familiarity, I was able to be more confident and effectively overcome these challenges.

While it has been frustrating to navigate through life with a learning disability and its disadvantages, such as not being able to do basic things with my hands as easily as others, I have not allowed it to weigh me down. I found the strength to ask for help when I needed it and to take what others taught me and make it my own. That way I can reach my potential, and not see myself as weak. If I can find the strength to admit my limitations and find a way to overcome them, you can too.

Chapter 3: Spatial Perception Difficulties

S patial perception difficulties were a third hurdle I had to cross. I have trouble interpreting spatial relationships between my body and the environment around me. This made it significantly harder when learning to drive a car. To be a proficient driver, one needs to know how to use the many controls on the vehicle panel. On top of that, I have a poor sense of direction and struggled with differentiating north, south, east, and west. Unable to distinguish these points of reference made it even more difficult for me. My struggles in identifying directions combined with my impaired fine motor skills had me at a severe disadvantage compared to others.

There were other life skills I struggled with outside of the classroom due to my impaired spatial perception. One of those was passing the driving test to get my driver's license. I didn't pass my first time out. So, I worked even harder with my parents to improve my chances. When there were no vast improvements in my driving skills, such as parallel parking and driving in reverse, my parents decided to find me a driving instructor. Someone I had never met before who could offer a variety of new techniques and a different perspective. After a couple weeks with the instructor, I passed the driving test on my second attempt! I'm now an excellent driver. This shows how I did not let the ADD label control me or bring me down.

The first way in which I tackled this difficulty, aware that I am more of a visual learner, was to recall past experiences and use them to my advantage. Throughout my schooling, rather than simply being told how to complete a task or understand what was expected of me, I benefited more when I was shown how to do something in a visual step-by-step approach. I asked my teachers and others to model the task a couple of times before I did it independently. Simply by seeing someone else do it, I was filled with self-confidence that I could do it myself. I applied that principle to driving a car by depending on landmarks or familiar routes that I had used time and time again. Familiarity with my route allowed for an enhanced level of self-confidence when it came to navigating to a desired location.

In addition, I used the electronic compass on my dashboard. This mechanism told me what direction I was driving. Therefore, I could more easily follow a set of directions someone gave me. This device has helped me countless times. To whoever invented this technology, I owe you a huge thank you. I now find it much easier to get from one place to the next.

The third and final strategy I used was the GPS on my cell phone. If I didn't have a GPS, I would be lost, especially when I need to drive to a place that I haven't been to before. Once I become more familiar with the best route to take, I can depend less on the GPS. For example, a couple times a year I visit some of my best friends who I met during college in Charleston, Illinois, and still live in that area. The first few times I made the trip, I had to put the address into my phone. However, after driving there so often and becoming more familiar with my driving route, the last few times driving there I haven't had to rely on my phone's GPS. This proves the more and more you accomplish a task, the greater your confidence, and the less you need to depend on special accommodations.

Chapter 4: Communication Difficulties

With my ADD learning disability, sometimes I have found it hard to communicate with others. There were times when I saw frustration on the faces of family and friends because the response to a simple yes or no question was taking forever. Their wait was because I was anxious. That anxiety caused an inner struggle to find the right words. Momentarily, I felt like a mute while attempting to find a way to articulate an intelligent response. By doing that, I made it harder than it had to be. After all, some of the time I just needed to say yes or no. Yet, I complicated it and made myself nervous.

Possibly the single biggest factor that caused communication problems was my shyness. While it did not help that I had a high level of nervousness, I am also quite shy. These two negative side effects of my learning disability make it extremely difficult to communicate. At times when my words do not come out quick enough, I then speak in a softer tone. So, sometimes it is harder to hear me and to understand what I am saying. As a result, the way I communicate with others has been negatively impacted.

To overcome this difficulty, I have relied on writing down my thoughts and feelings. I express myself much easier in written form as opposed to speaking. Take this book for example. Simply by writing this book, after all these years with the various accommodations, therapy sessions, and so much more, I am finally able to communicate my thoughts and feelings about how this learning disability has affected me and my relationships with others. There is absolutely no way I'd have the confidence to say this otherwise. To those who have a learning disability, I implore you to not let any communication difficulties impede you. Instead, be like me, and find alternative ways to navigate through life. I will not lie to you and say it's an easy task. It has taken me years to not only accept my uniqueness, but to embrace it, and to finally, with the help of others, come up with creative ways to strive for success in society. Find your own voice! I am living proof that it can be done.

Chapter 5: Social Skills Difficulties

My learning disability has hindered my ability to understand social cues. As a result of some limitations in social skills, I struggled to make friends. Luckily, when I went to college at EIU, things started to get better for me. I met some of the nicest people who are still good friends of mine even fifteen years later. Some of them still live in Central Illinois, while others live as far as Kansas City, Missouri. I miss them a lot, especially because I have a limited number of friendships with people who live near me in the Oak Park area.

Even though my long-distance friends are not as close geographically, we are still close emotionally. The first friend I made in college was Andy. Andy and I met in an introductory English Literature class. It was such a fun class. We watched episodes of *Simpsons* and wrote journal responses about the episodes. That wasn't the only part of the class, but it is one of the most memorable.

Andy is a computer guy. He was my go-to tech support guy. While Andy taught me about different operating systems, I taught him about theatre and sports, especially baseball. It all started because Andy knew how much of a Chicago Cubs fan I was, and to be a good friend, he asked to learn more about this interest of mine. Since Andy hadn't watched a lot of baseball, I taught him all the rules. Once, he got so animated, yelling how the batter should be out if he fouled the ball while there were two strikes. I explained to him that would only occurs if the batter bunts. Andy then asked what a *bunt* is. Oh, those were good times with Andy! We would continue to learn many things from each other over the course of our friendship.

A year into our friendship, Andy met his future wife, Victoria. Victoria and Andy first met at a church gathering, which turned out great for Andy because attending church is an important part of his life. They are perfect for each other.

Andy & Victoria

Victoria also became a good friend of mine, partly because we bonded while constantly talking about the Chicago Cubs. Every once in a while, she texts me to see how I'm doing. By the way, thank you Victoria for making Andy such an enthusiastic Cubs fan.

Since Andy and Victoria now live quite a distance from me, I am unable to catch up with them as often as I would like. Sometimes I wish we had time to communicate as we did before, especially Andy and me. But with our busy work schedules, it just doesn't work out that way. At the very least, we wish each other a happy birthday and send greetings on holidays. I hope that one day Andy and I can be as close as we were all those years ago.

Besides Andy and Victoria, there were several other friendships that formed at EIU. One of the life-long friends I met was Courtney. She lives a couple of hours away in the Central Illinois area with her husband, Greg. They are proud parents of a lovely baby girl, Amelia. Unfortunately, due to the Coronavirus, I was not able to meet Amelia in person until she was one and a half years old. Until then, I had to rely on the adorable pictures that Courtney and Greg posted on Facebook. Though the pandemic made it difficult to see Amelia in her early months, I am confident I'll spend more time with her now.

Courtney and I originally met through Andy. The fact that she was interested in theatre made it even easier for us to become friends and to talk with each other. She is such a loyal friend and will do almost anything to cheer me up when I feel sad.

On the flip side, she has a wonderfully contagious laugh that makes you so happy, you can't help but giggle yourself. I remember a particularly funny night when Courtney, Lyndsey, and I went out for drinks. On this night, a woman who we'd never met before walked up to us at the bar and began to tell us her whole life story, including why it's so important to pick a major. Courtney started to giggle. Lyndsey and I tried with all our might to bite our tongues. When Courtney's laugh got louder, I couldn't hold mine inside anymore, and it burst out, which, of course, caused Lyndsey to laugh as well. Unfortunately, the lady got mad because she thought we were making fun of her, and she abruptly left. The three of us continued to chuckle uncontrollably for at least five minutes more.

Courtney's sense of humor is like no other. This allows us to easily have fun together. Whether we go to a bar, a Cubs game, or anywhere else, she and I have a blast.

Courtney & me

Courtney and I have been friends for so long in part because we both love theatre and the performing arts. Courtney always lets me know when she is involved in a community theatre performance, and I use that as a reason to go and visit her. When we do not see each other in person, we keep in touch through texting. Courtney also checks up on me if we have not communicated in a few weeks. Sometimes she contacts me if she's going through a bad patch and needs to talk to a good friend. More than once, Courtney and I have commented on how we are so close that at times it's like we are brother and sister.

Coincidentally, it was Courtney who told me, more than once during the first few months of our friendship, how she thought I was going to go on and do big things. How I would make a difference! I think she meant in theatre, not book-writing. Still, Courtney you were right! I remember that wonderful compliment because it's just as heart-warming now, as it was when she first said it all those years ago.

The third friend I met while at EIU was Lyndsey. Now, much like Courtney, Lyndsey also lives a couple of hours away in the Central Illinois area. She and Courtney live a few minutes away from each other. Lyndsey also has a lovely family, with her husband, Chris, and their amazing two sons, Malcolm and Sebastian. I have had the great opportunity to watch the two boys grow up, and how lucky they are to have such wonderful parents.

When I first met Lyndsey, she was roommates with Courtney. She was involved in marching band. Her love of music and the arts gave us so much to talk about. We soon realized we had a lot in common. At that time, she wanted to become a music teacher, and I wanted to become a theatre teacher. She has achieved her goal and is currently a music teacher at a school close to her home. Since she is such a good friend, and she knows I am always looking for a teaching position, whenever she hears about any local teaching opportunities, she immediately lets me know. In fact, she told me about an open fourth-grade teaching position at her school. As it turned out, I was hired in January 2019, during the middle of the school year, because the previous teacher left. I was excited about this opportunity for several reasons, which included working with one of my best friends, being able to teach my favorite

grade, and to again live in the Central Illinois area as I had while I attended EIU. While there, Lyndsey and I had a great time working together.

Like my friendship with Courtney, Lyndsey and I text a lot, and we can talk about almost anything. In fact, I believe she is the one friend I text with the most. While I don't get to see her as much as I would like to, I always enjoy her company. However, we make a point of seeing each other once year….at Wrigley Field. Over the last few years, we have started a tradition. Every summer she drives the few hours to Chicago so we can go see a Cubs game together.

Lyndsey & me at Wrigley Field

Lyndsey and her husband, Chris, like to brag about how they made me into a gamer like them. In addition, they increased my understanding and appreciation for the *Star Wars* films. I can remember watching the original trilogy with my family when I was younger, and I saw the first of the three prequel films when it was in the theater. Back then, I didn't understand the plot. Now, thanks to Lyndsey, I'm more knowledgeable about the *Star Wars* saga. However, I am not a die-hard fan. Sorry, Lyndsey. You were not successful in that regard.

After years of friendship and working together, Lyndsey and I realized why the two of us clicked instantly at college and have remained so close. We have overlapping interests in promoting the arts, in seeing the importance of education in a young child's life, and in cheering for the Chicago Cubs. In addition, she, and I both go through life with an elevated level of anxiety, which is something we talk about together.

Obviously, I have been friends with Courtney and Lyndsey for many years. We all met at college and graduated from EIU together. And we have remained friends, proving that some friendships will last a very long time. That is something that I wouldn't have believed prior to attending EIU, due to my difficulties making friends, and in part due to my ADD diagnosis.

Do not worry, my Oak Park friends, I have not forgotten about you. My best friend in the Oak Park area, which is my hometown, is Chris.

Chris

We have been friends ever since high school. Chris and I like to see movies, watch WWE wresting, go to Cubs games, bowl, or whatever else sounds like fun. I always enjoy hanging out with Chris. I believe Chris is a true friend. Chris is someone I can contact if I'm having trouble assembling furniture due to my fine motor difficulties. He is very handy with tools. I cannot begin to tell you how comforting it is to know I have a friend who knows about my fine motor issues and is happy to help me. That is an excellent friend!

I can tell him just about anything, and he wouldn't judge me. In that way, he is just like my friends from Central Illinois. While Chris lives closer in distance, that doesn't mean finding time to hang out together comes any easier. Chris works two jobs, and I am busy with what I am doing, so there are sometimes huge gaps in time when we don't get to see each other. But when our schedules free up and when we can meet, we have a great time.

Chris is another friend who celebrates the Chicago Cubs with me often. We have made it to many games at Wrigley and continue to go as frequently as we can. A couple of times, for my birthday in September, Chris has treated me to a Cubs game. When we go to Cubs games on days other than my birthday, I pay for my ticket and half the price of parking. But on my birthday, Chris doesn't allow me to pay, no matter how many times I offer.

One memorable moment occurred when we had possibly the best seats I'd ever had at a Cubs game. We were just a few rows from the dugout on the third base side. I really got my money's worth with the memorabilia I was able to collect. During the game, I met Braun Strowman, one of my favorite WWE superstars. Meeting Strowman happened merely by coincidence on so many levels. At first, we were unsure that it was him. All we saw, a few rows to the right from where we were seated, was a tall, muscular guy who looked like a serious weightlifter. We noticed him, not just because of his immense size, but because he was being applauded by others who were seated next to him. While other people where we were seated were completely oblivious to who he was, Chris and I commented to each other how much he looked like Strowman. It was at this point that Chris found out, through social media on his cell phone, that Strowman was at the same Cubs game. He had posted an invitation to any fan there to drop by for a photo. Chris and I decided we could not let this opportunity slip by without getting a photo with him. We approached him at different times because we didn't want him to feel like he was being overwhelmed by a swarm of nerdy fans.

I remember being so nervous about meeting him. I could hardly handle my cell phone because I was so excited. Normally, I can hold my phone for taking a selfie. That is a feat, considering my issues with limited fine motor skills. However, the fact that Strowman was a celebrity, and that I had not been this close to someone so famous caused me overwhelming joy. Strowman, being the gentleman he is, took the selfie himself.

If taking a selfie with a celebrity like Strowman was not enough, later I was able to get an autograph from one of the Cubs players. After the game, many people went to the front row, where one of the players was signing autographs. As I got to the front, I realized it was Ben Zobrist. That made me excited to get his autograph. After all, to Cubs fans Zobrist is a big hero. He is the one who got the big hit in extra innings that broke the tied score during game seven of the 2016 World Series. Thereby, he set in motion an event that took over a hundred years for die-hard Cubs fans to experience…the Cubs winning the World Series! I asked Zobrist to sign the baseball cap I wore to the game. That cap is now in a protective case displayed proudly in my bedroom.

While this game ranks high on my "most memorable" list, there is another one I also remember vividly. Chris called to invite me to a game as I was returning home from a religious service on the Jewish High Holy Day of Rosh Hashanah. It is an important holiday that I have observed my entire life due to having been raised in an inter-faith household. For the Jewish faith, Rosh Hashanah celebrates the beginning of the New Year.

Because it is such an important holiday, I had two conflicting thoughts after Chris invited me to the ballgame. First, as a huge Cubs fan, I thought "Hell yeah!" However, my second thought was guilt about not spending the whole day with my family. In the past, our family celebrated Rosh Hashanah by going to synagogue and then sitting together for a holiday meal.

Luckily the conflict of emotions I was experiencing did not last long because my mom and dad, overhearing the phone call, urged me to go. They said, "Why not start a new year with a Cubs win? Then come home and we will be together." That shows how cool my parents are.

Once I got approval, I quickly changed from my dressy suit to casual Cubs apparel. Then Chris and I went to Wrigley Field to see the Cubs win. This game was so memorable that every year on High Holidays, I remember the one time I was able to both celebrate Rosh Hashanah and watch the Cubs win. My strong Jewish identity and being a die-hard Cubs fan are two prominent characteristics that define me.

Friendships have made quite a positive impact on my life. They have shown me that some strong bonds will never be broken. Each one of them has taught me how to be a good friend. Andy taught me to think about your friends' interests. Even if it's something that may not be all that fascinating to you. Like the way I listened when he talked about computer programs and how much he enjoys helping others by fixing their computers. Likewise, he watched a few baseball games with me. This give-and-take approach to friendship is a good reason why Andy and I have remained close friends for so many years. Thank you, Andy.

Lyndsey taught me the pros and cons of being the type of person who puts everyone else's health and happiness before their own. Both she and I must be certain everyone else is settled before we can sit and relax. While that is a good thing, I've learned the negative impact it can have. When one is so worried about everyone but themselves, it can be a bit overwhelming. In fact, it can be so much that one keeps inside all the emotions they may be going through and out of pure exhaustion, doesn't communicate to their loved ones. Eventually, doing this for so long can lead to some sort of mental break. I know because one day I had to help Lyndsey when she was having an episode. Luckily, we were working together at the time. She texted me to come see her because she needed help. I literally ran over to help my friend in need. Lyndsey told me how a minor side comment had her doubting how good a teacher she was. It triggered her doubt because there was a lot that she was holding within. I hugged her as tight as I could and told her encouraging things to boost her self-esteem and confidence.

It tore my heart that she allowed herself to feel like a failure. But seeing what it did to Lyndsey was a wake-up call. Once I saw in-person that holding in your anger, sadness, or whatever emotion you are feeling, can cause an implosion, I wanted to avoid experiencing a similar feeling. I wouldn't have discovered the importance if it were not for Lyndsey. Thank you, Lyndsey.

My friend, Courtney, taught me that it is okay to find joy in the small moments. While I am shy, Courtney is outgoing and more of a risk-taker. At times, she has convinced me at times to do things I normally wouldn't do. For example, going on outdoor hikes, camping trips or other outdoor activities. I am an indoor person at heart. Due to her insistence, Courtney taught me it is okay to take risks as long as they make you happy. Now, I can sometimes have a little spontaneity in my life. Thank you, Courtney.

Lastly, Chris is the person who has taught me the importance of being a dependable friend. Whenever I've felt sad or drained either mentally or emotionally, he is one of the first people I contact. Chris is the kind of friend that would do anything for you in your time of need. He will drop everything and come running to you to provide comfort, so you don't have to feel one more second of despair. In other words, he is reliable. That makes for a long-lasting friendship. Thank you, Chris.

All these friendships have taught me characteristics of what makes up a true friend. To share a bond over another friend's passion, be an effective communicator, be more spontaneous, and be reliable. I have tried to take on n these qualities, and it has made me a better person. For that, I thank every one of you.

Part Three: Characteristics of a Disability

My ADD has definitely shaped my identity. However, I do not see the disability as a "mountain to climb". On the contrary, this diagnosis has shaped me into an individual who knows that obstacles can be overcome. I've learned the characteristics resulting from ADD do not necessarily have to be a bad thing. These traits, which I will lay out in the next several chapters, can be seen in a positive way. Once I realized that life-lesson, I was able to say the following sentence with pride- I am Paul Elliot Martin, and I have a learning disability!

Chapter 1: Repetitive

Possibly one of the most important characteristics of mine is the tendency to favor repetition. This stems from having to find creative ways or accommodations to adapt to the limitations brought on by my ADD learning disability. I have been encouraged and supported by many people. My family, many teachers and other professionals have helped by making suggestions and ideas on how to succeed academically. Throughout the years, there were many ideas offered, and while some were proven effective, the most influential idea was to keep a steady and repetitive routine. It was suggested, based on observations of how I perform in the classroom and at home, that with a sense of familiarity came a boost to my self-confidence.

Enforcing this "same old, same old" approach in school was shown to be a successful strategy. All the adults who advocated for repetition were correct in how to boost my scholastic achievements. I performed better in the classroom when I felt a sense of familiarity with a task. The more I repeated something, the more it became etched in my mind. As a result, I gained self-confidence, received phenomenal grades, and was regarded as one of the best students. During my middle school and high school years, aided by the special accommodations employed by the schools, I was consistently on the Dean's List and Honor Roll. To be on that list, I earned a grade point average (GPA) of 3.5 or higher out of a 4.0 scale. Having such a high GPA continued into my college years. I graduated from EIU with a Bachelor of Arts degree in theatre with a 3.4 GPA, and later graduated from Concordia University, Chicago, with a Master of Arts degree in teaching with a 4.0 GPA.

I implemented this need to have repetition in my life outside the classroom as well. Much like I can watch a movie or TV show from my extensive DVD collection hundreds of times, I can also adhere to the same strict daily schedule for months, or years, on end. I keep much of my life at a constant so there is little element of surprise. That is why I like to stick to as stringent a schedule as possible. Having a sense of familiarity has helped with such activities as following driving routes, planning weekly errands/events, and so on. By maintaining structure in my life, I've been able to prevent the element of surprise to the best of my ability. However, it is not a 100 percent certainty. Particularly because life can be disrupted by any possible unforeseen event. Take this recent deadly, global Coronavirus outbreak, for example. Since I am a substitute teacher, when the schools closed, I lost my job for an extended period of time. This dilemma introduced a drastic change in my lifestyle. I had to create a new daily schedule as a way of putting routine in my life while I was unemployed.

Take this lesson from my experiences. Find a routine that suits you but be ready to adapt it from time to time. Having a plan and order of things has helped me remain calm. However, the world is not so orderly. Therefore, I must always find a way to be flexible. Be like me, and have a plan B in your pocket, so to speak.

Chapter 2: Protective Mode

A direct result of having a limiting disability is the unwanted sympathy one receives from others. That is why I don't immediately offer the information that I have ADD. Normally, the loved ones and friends I can trust are the only ones who know. In other words, this piece of information is not something I like to advertise around someone I don't know. For instance, I wouldn't mention it at a job interview, though I may communicate it to the people I work with at a later time.

Why don't I offer this information right away? The answer is simple. I don't want unnecessary sympathy or to be seen as weak. Furthermore, I don't want to succeed because of special treatment. I have never used my limitations as a crutch or an excuse, and I've never shirked my responsibilities causing more work for someone else. That isn't my style. I am someone who sees myself as independent and who likes to try things on my own. On many occasions, I have refused offers from others to step in and help instead of allowing me to try it by myself first. This comes from my mindset of determination to defy all odds, to prove I can do anything someone without a disability can do, perhaps even do it better.

Do not get me wrong. I am not someone who can't ask for assistance. My pride doesn't get in the way of my determination regarding asking others for help when I need it. There is absolutely nothing wrong with failing and then pulling yourself back up and asking for someone to help you get done what you couldn't do on your own. But I do want to try it on my own first. Failure is a part of life that we all experience at one time or another. Like everybody else, I need to learn how to cope with failure, pick myself up, and learn from my mistakes.

The example I provided above about initially concealing my learning disability from others is what I have termed my "protective mode." I use this self-created safety mechanism to avoid being seen as weak. To me, this is the best defense to prevent the unwanted sympathy people might want to bestow upon me after learning that I have ADD. I've pinpointed when this "protective mode" first occurred—it was in March of 2007. Allow me to set the stage for you. I was a senior in high school and received the sad news that my grandmother passed away. It was a devastating loss. I was about to graduate high school, and I was so sad to realize that I wouldn't get to celebrate this milestone with my grandma.

Also, in the months leading up to March 2007, I was trying my best to avoid the very tough decision of ending a close friendship that lasted many years. I had been friends with this person since the fourth grade. However, he started to change and began hanging out with some people who I thought were steering him in the wrong direction. Then a series of unpleasant events started to happen. First, we'd make plans. Second, he'd no-show. Third, he'd apologize. Fourth, I'd forgive him. This negative cycle occurred every time I wanted to do something with my good friend.

Not only was the duration of our friendship a major factor in my inability to separate from him, but it was also the fact he kept apologizing. I believed he took responsibility and owned up to his mistakes, making me think he saw the importance of our friendship. For those reasons, I gave him second chance after second chance. It is possible this was because I was raised to give people an opportunity to redeem themselves. As justification for clinging onto the friendship, I abided by my upbringing and the faith that he would eventually come around and see the mistakes he was making. Unfortunately, that never happened.

Being unable to separate from my friend speaks volumes about my loyalty. Even though I had problems of my own, I tried to be as supportive as I could be. My ADD caused many problems for me academically, mentally, and emotionally. However, it didn't stop me from caring for this friend. We had been through a lot, and I felt that I couldn't simply abandon our friendship. Maybe it was noble of me because of my huge heart. On the other hand, maybe I was naïve. Either way, I found it difficult to simply end our friendship. I refused to believe that there was not a part of him that still felt the same about our friendship as I did.

Then a remarkable thing happened. The friend approached me once he found out about my grandma passing. He assured me that he would attend my grandmother's funeral to help support me. I thought it had finally happened- I had my best friend back. Sadly, he didn't show up. That was the last straw. I decided I wasn't giving him another opportunity to let me down like he had for the last year or so.

That incident affected me in a big way. After losing what I thought was such a good friend, I told myself I would not display my vulnerability ever again. That is when "protective mode" started to play a major role in my decision-making. Many times, I refused assistance from others.

Allowing myself to be in "protective mode" has caused more harm than good. More times than I can honestly remember, I talked myself out of things or delayed crucial decisions. The delay was because of fear. Not fear of failure, but more a fear of rejection and the depression it may cause. To me, there is a big difference. So, to prevent the possibility of rejection as best I can, I enter "protective mode." Before doing things like applying for a job, asking a woman out on a date, or any other "risky" situations, I become analytical, weighing the pros and cons.

Speaking of asking a woman on a date, I think that is the single biggest defeat that "protective mode" has caused. Since dating in its very nature, requires both participants to have a level of vulnerability I've avoided it. So, two contrary things are happening. In my heart, I want to be close to someone and have an emotional connection. However, my brain is being analytical and causing my "protective mode" to take over. In my opinion, if I allow myself to enter "protective mode" when considering asking a woman out, it won't happen. That is why I need to decrease my dependency on that phase so it will not be as strong, and therefore, I'll be more comfortable taking the risk of asking a lovely lady out.

Yet, I cannot put my inability to have a meaningful romantic relationship all on "protective mode." There are other contributing factors that may explain why I have been disappointed many times in this specific area of life. First, there are some side effects from my ADD learning disability diagnosis. For instance, communication with others has been a life-long struggle. Being able to talk with a woman and express how I feel is very difficult. I always find it quite intimidating to tell a woman that she is pretty and that I am attracted to her. As a result, I allow a level of fear to creep in when the opportunity presents itself. Fear that I will be rejected. Or even worse, laughed at. This fear negatively impacts my self-confidence and causes me to doubt myself. As a result, there are many times that I don't express my feelings to this day.

Another reason I've had difficulty in finding a life partner is because of the self-sabotage I put myself through. I convince myself there is no way a woman as great as she is, could be interested in a guy like me. In other words, I never even give myself a chance. I regret the number of times I have done that.

To overcome these obstacles, I've started online dating. In a way, the variety of sites that I have tried have decreased the level of pressure and have allowed me to feel more comfortable in reaching out to a woman. As a part of the online dating process, I first read a person's profile, and after determining how compatible I think we are, I reach out to her. Then we chat for a few days. This affords me the chance to get to know her better while not letting her see how nervous I am. After a few days of this communication, my nerves start to disappear, and I feel comfortable enough to ask if she wants to meet in-person. Using this method, I've been on a few dates. Certainly, more than before I started online dating.

Despite my increased dating, I've not found my special someone yet. However, I continue to be optimistic. One day, I will meet that special person to have a family with. I remain positive because all the women I meet tell me what a nice guy I am. Many of them say, "You are a nice guy, but…" You can probably infer the rest of the sentence. While I'm growing a little tired of hearing that line, I remain confident that one day it will eventually all change. How one day, the "but" in the statement will be erased, and with it, my years of frustration. I try to think this way for my own sake. Instead of letting doubt and disappointment reach a climax, I will eventually meet the woman of my dreams, whomever and wherever she may be.

I am constantly trying to find a balance, so I do not allow the disadvantages of "protective mode" to cause me to enter self-sabotage. Thereby, proving that some coping mechanisms can be unhealthy. Those who live in a similar situation, I implore you to take comfort in knowing that you are not the only one. While it does little to give you an answer on how to solve the problem, I sincerely hope you can take solace in the fact that there are others like you.

Chapter 3: Anxious

Currently, hundreds of thousands of people suffer from anxiety. With the trillions of dollars we spend on medical care, we still haven't made enough progress when it comes to treatment for mental illness. Do yourself a favor and ignore the people who tell you mental health isn't a high medical concern. On the contrary, there are many people close to me who have a high level of anxiety. So, when I see people, even elected officials in our government, downplaying the importance of mental health reform, it irritates me on a personal level. Then I ask myself a series of questions: 1) Do these people know what they are talking about? 2) Have they ever visited a mental hospital and witnessed the variety of problems? 3) Are they not aware of all the money people spend on medications and therapy? 4) Are they ignorant of facts, ignoring data, or just not aware of the situation? Whatever the case, I implore those individuals, while it's perfectly okay to have an opinion, if you have little or no experience with mental health issues, then this is one time that you should shut your mouth. Like one of my favorite WWE wrestlers, Dwayne "The Rock" Johnson used to say, "Know your role and shut your mouth."

I am one of those people who suffers from anxiety. My level of anxiety is heightened by my learning disability. Throughout my schooling, I put additional pressure on myself to succeed academically. My disability forced me to work two, maybe three times harder than others in the class without the limitations I had. I wanted to show I could do anything despite the diagnosis. A noble and inspiring thing to do, but it has come at a price. Due to this added pressure, I put stress on myself. Probably too much. Even now, it is hard to decrease the level of pressure I instinctively put on myself, but it's something that I work on every day.

I remember a most stressful time in my life that caused great anxiety. I was thirteen years old and preparing for my Bar Mitzvah. A Bar Mitzvah is the incredibly special occasion in a Jewish child's life when they publicly read a Hebrew excerpt from the Holy Torah, and, according to the Jewish law, become an adult. This event was basically the culmination of years of Sunday School and Hebrew instruction at my local synagogue.

While my Bar Mitzvah in October of 2001 was a memorable event in my life, it was also a difficult time. A couple months earlier, in August my mom had an unexpected health scare involving her heart. She had to have quadruple bypass open heart surgery. It was a scary and traumatic day. Both my brother and I were home at the time. She went to see her doctor early in the day because she felt weak. At the doctor's office, everything checked out fine. But when she got home and started to go upstairs to take a nap, she felt a lot of pressure in her chest. I called an ambulance, my brother checked on her, and my dad left work to meet my mom at the hospital. While this was happening, I tried my best to stay on schedule with my Hebrew readings for my upcoming Bar Mitzvah. It was difficult to concentrate, though. Soon, my dad called and gave us an update. Apparently, after a series of tests in the emergency room, it was revealed that she was having a heart attack. She was stabilized and then scheduled for bypass surgery the next day.

This event was alarming to everyone involved. My mom, while worried for her own health, was even more concerned about making it to my Bar Mitzvah, which was to occur six weeks later. It was reported that during the surgery, she talked about how she needed to be at my Bar Mitzvah. The doctor assured her she would recover and dance at her son's special event. That is the kind of person my mom is. She puts so much emphasis on being a part of important events in people's lives.

A month later, after my mom had already come home from the hospital, a devastating day occurred in American history. It was September 11, 2001, the day the Twin Towers in New York City and other governmental landmark sites in the United States were attacked. Thankfully, my mom had company with her while she was watching this event transpire during her recovery. Grandma Nana was with her because this was the first day that my dad had returned to work in downtown Chicago after staying at home to care for my mom.

During the first few minutes of the 9/11 attack, there was much confusion. After the first plane collided into the World Trade Center, no one knew if it was deliberate. There were questions of a mechanical failure with the plane. Then, the moment the second plane dove into the building, everything changed. At that moment, there was no doubt anymore. My mom always tells the story of how she and Nana were watching it live on TV. Once they witnessed the second plane hit the World Trade Center, they looked at each other and said, "This was no accident." They were not the only ones who had this reaction. Everyone knew it was an attack but didn't know how many other targets were out there. Immediately, there was an overall increased sense of panic.

Although I did not see either plane hit the buildings, I still remember exactly where I was during both events. During the first plane crash, I'd just left for school and had reached my bus stop. When I arrived at school, the second plane had just hit.

My mom and Nana were worried on so many levels. My brother and I had already left for school, Josh at high school and me at middle school. In addition, my dad was on his way to work in downtown Chicago, a highly populated area. And since New York was being attacked, people were worried that other cities like Chicago would be under attack as well.

Possibly the most shocking thing I remember about 9/11 was seeing the replay of the Two Towers collapsing on live TV. I mean, it was something out of an action movie, but it was real-life. That made it even more eye-opening.

My mom's surgery and witnessing such a horrific attack on our country occurred within a short amount of time. Those would have been a lot to deal with on their own, much less right before my Bar Mitzvah. Though my family and the world were still healing from the harrowing events of the fall of 2001, we all came together to celebrate on the day of my Bar Mitzvah, finding that joy and love were just what we needed.

From the moment I turned thirteen up to the present-day, I've been the more anxious type of person. At times, my anxiousness has worried my family. While they try to be supportive, some phrases they say, I don't appreciate. When they say things like, "It's not that bad" or "Don't worry so much" I get irritated. It is not as if they do not care. I know they do. But statements like that sometimes rub me the wrong way. In response to my frustration, my family has become very selective with the words and phrases they use to console me.

While some rationalizations don't help, one phrase that has made a positive difference to me is, "You can only control your reaction and how you cope." In other words, some situations may be out of my control, but I can control my reaction to the situation and try not to get so upset. My parents, as well as the therapist I am currently seeing, have told me that. The more I hear the phrase, the more I see the wisdom in it.

Chapter 4: Honor my Commitments

D o you know someone who tells others that their word is their bond? That is me to a tee. I don't make false commitments or promises. If I say that I will do something, then I will. A good example of my need to honor my commitments took place in my first year of high school. At that time, I thought I would give wrestling a shot and decided to try out for the team. I was a member of the team for only one season. Honestly, I wasn't a great wrestler. This was partly because the other students on the team had more experience. Also, I was less agile due to poor motor skills from my ADD. I won a couple of matches, but I did not have the killer instinct that others on the team possessed.

Eventually, the number of hours required to practice was taking its toll on me. I was starting to get sick. I saw my doctor at the time, and she offered me a way out. She said she'd be willing to write me a doctor's note to release me from the team. I refused the offer and wanted to stick it out for the rest of the season. This speaks to my persistence and loyalty. I am the kind of person who when I make a commitment or promise, I keep it. I can't remember a time when I broke a promise. Keeping my word is important to me.

Speaking of promises, I made one to that doctor many years ago. She made me swear that if I were to stop wrestling, I would find something else I loved participating in that would be worth all the hours I put into it. The following year, I began to participate in backstage theatre as an assistant crew member. Backstage theatre requires a lot of time, but it is surely something I love to do. I kept my promise. In addition, I understood the point my doctor was trying to make- accept that certain things aren't for you and let go of them to make room for something better.

Another way I keep my word is to be present when I say I will. If I tell anyone that I will be there, I will be. And on time, if not early. I believe that if someone is awaiting my arrival, it is much better to be early rather than late. That said, there have been multiple occasions when I arrive at a destination maybe a little too early. This mentality is a result of an experience when I went to a Cubs game with my entire family. While my mom and brother had a more relaxed, "we'll get there when we get there" mentality, my dad and I were more rushed. Sure enough, when we got to the stadium, the game had already started. The feeling of being so anxious the entire drive is a feeling I vowed to avoid at all costs. As a result, I always leave extra time when driving to any destination.

I have used this attitude about time to my advantage. For instance, when I've worked as stage manager for a theatre company. The general rule is for a stage manager to arrive a few minutes early to rehearsal so that they can help set up the space, as well as to meet with the director or anyone else beforehand. Therefore, when the actors and actresses arrive, everything is ready. Having this sort of attitude about arriving early, it has helped make me an effective stage manager.

I take my words seriously and always honor my commitments. Of course, I've had to learn how to make sure I also consider my own health. This quality of standing by my word is one that I take pride in.

Chapter 5: Listen to Others

One prominent characteristic that defines me is that I'm an excellent listener. In my opinion, that is in large part due to my ADD learning disability. With a learning disability, and all the struggles that I have had to overcome because of it, I couldn't have succeeded without the emotional support from my family and the academic support from my teachers. I feel they took my best interests into consideration and determined the appropriate strategies to help me reach my greatest academic potential. Yes, technically that was a requirement by law for my teachers because I had an IEP. However, I felt everyone went the extra mile. That inspired me to do the same for myself and others.

As a teacher, I go the extra mile for my students by making sure to listen intently. When I introduce myself and go over my expectations, I let them know that if anyone has a question or anything to tell me, they can be sure they'll have my full attention. By implementing this rule, I am invoking mutual respect in the classroom. The students respect me by waiting for their turn, and I respect them by giving them my absolute, undivided attention. Whether it be a full-time permanent teaching position, or as a substitute teacher, I distinctly communicate this expectation.

Being a teacher is very important to me. I love to advocate for the next generation. Especially those in my classroom with a learning disability. With my advocacy and personal experiences, I can help implement strategies and accommodations that will help them reach their potential. Helping students just like my teachers did while I was a student, brings a smile to my face.

My willingness to advocate for another person comes easily. When someone shares how they are going through a hard time, my level of caring and empathy takes over, and it is as if I'm going through it with them. I am an excellent ally, as I will do almost anything to support someone I care about. On the other end of the spectrum, I'm a fierce opponent or foe. If you screw me or anyone I care about, I'm determined to right the wrong. For example, when my brother, Josh, was having a hard time getting medication because of insurance issues, I stepped in to help him. I called the doctors and the insurance companies to explain the urgency of the matter. My brother needed his medication right away. I understood the logistics of what had to happen to get it to him. I clearly communicated the importance and urgency of the situation to the person on the other end of the phone. Through my persistence, I was able to get Josh a short-term supply until the loose ends were worked out, such as how much insurance would cover and other exciting details like that. I have done similar acts for my mom and dad as well. I will never allow someone I care for to feel as if they are being taken advantage of.

My level of empathy and desire to advocate for others are major effects of my learning disability. I will never forget those special people who have kept my best interests at heart. The accommodations that were fought for and implemented made a great difference in my life. Thanks to all that was done especially for me, I was able to meet, and even exceed the bar that was set for me. Therefore, I feel I owe a favor to those who were so helpful. In my own way, I am repaying the debt I owe. Now, I know those people will try to assure me that repayment isn't necessary, but no matter how hard they try, it's how I feel.

Chapter 6: Curiosity in Other Cultures

My curiosity has complemented my learning disability. It has fed my love of learning and schooling, and it inspired me to live in the moment. I was eager to learn more about my community, as well as different cultures around the world. During my high school years, I asked myself how I could seize the moment, and it came to me—by travelling the world! This was a rather easy goal to enact because, at the time, my parents also liked to travel, and they had the means to do it. I especially love all the wonderful experiences I've had in Italy.

I have been to Italy three times: twice with my family and once when I participated in a study abroad program in Florence, Italy during my third year of college. The experience was one of the best times of my life. On school days, I enjoyed walking along the Arno River on my way to class. And I enjoyed looking at all the beautiful architecture and history surrounding me. During those times, I just felt like I was at peace.

I also appreciated how people in Italy, and other European countries, are more leisurely than Americans. They take their time when walking from place to place, sitting down for a meal, and enjoying one another's company. In the middle of the day, the restaurants and stores close for three to four hours, and then reopen for the evening. It requires a different mindset, but as a result, not as much stress as we put on ourselves in the U.S.A.

While it has been a while since I visited Italy, I still practice my Italian language skills. Any chance I get, I review all I learned from my high school courses, and from visiting Italy. For instance, when there was a shutdown due to the Coronavirus pandemic, I started to use an app on my phone called Duolingo. Not only did I use Duolingo to review my Italian skills, but I also met a goal of mine- to learn Portuguese. That was something I had thought of doing for many years, but never did. Since the app had the feature of allowing you to switch from one language to another, I thought it was the perfect time to finally learn Portuguese.

What makes Duolingo such a valuable foreign language instruction application is that it combines both visual and auditory learning styles to appeal to those with different learning proficiencies. Not to mention the fact that Duolingo makes learning a lot of fun! And for those with a competitive spirit, you can compete against other learners and jockey for positions on a leader board.

I recommend you learn a foreign language and travel to the country where that language is spoken. Do not let people tell you that because you have a disability you cannot take advantage of the opportunity to travel. Instead, listen to someone who learned Italian and visited its homeland. I plan to do the same once again with the Portuguese language. Portugal, here I come.

Spend time abroad and enjoy life by experiencing new and different cultures. Feed your curiosity. Never stifle it.

Chapter 7: Sense of Belonging

A huge part of my life is theatre arts. Being involved in theatre has always instilled in me a sense of purpose. To help illustrate this point, I refer you to a question that I've been asked more times than I can count: "Why do you like theatre so much?" The answer is: "Theatre has always given me a feeling of belonging." Working backstage in theatre productions has provided me an opportunity to be accepted by a group of my peers.

There are some people who think that performing in a play or movie requires the actor to become another character. To use that analogy, imagine being in school or at work for several hours a day and then attending a drama club or rehearsal afterwards. The person you are during the day is different from the one you are when engaged in a theatre performance. I have always felt that once I'm part of a show, I can take off the mask of the character I am playing during the school or workday who is required to follow the expectations of society. When drama club or rehearsal starts, I can figuratively remove the mask and transform into the person I actually am. Theatre allows me to be myself, Paul Elliot Martin.

Furthermore, theatre allows me to have a feeling of contentment. For example, at one point in my life, I had two jobs- one a substitute teacher in the western suburbs, and an assistant stage manager for a theater in downtown Chicago. Obviously, working two jobs created a level of exhaustion. On many occasions, the following happened: First, I was tired at the school I worked at, but plowed through and remained the professional I am. Second, I was tired on the drive going to the theater for my second job. Third, I suddenly got a boost of energy when I arrived at the theater and started rehearsal. Fourth, exhaustion hit again when I left the theater and was driving home for the night. That sequence of events proves that theatre creates a level of happiness and energy in me.

In my opinion, the performing arts is one of the most varied fields of cultural endeavor, allowing one to escape the stresses of everyday life. Its purpose could be to inform, enlighten, entertain, persuade, inspire, or evoke a variety of other human emotions. Theatre also fosters creativity and stimulates the imagination, and that is something we should never discourage, especially in children. If we do not encourage children to pursue their dreams and we stifle their creative spark, we are doing them a huge disservice.

For sure, we are better off with theatre than not. That being said, I remember when I was in college, I wrote a research paper about the marketability of jobs available in the theatre profession. Writing this paper was my reaction to being told over the years that a career in theatre was not financially rewarding, that I would be a starving artist, and that I could be homeless due to being unemployed. My family, meanwhile, was supportive when I wanted to pursue my dreams in theatre.

I only wish society could recognize the value in theatre arts like I do. Just look at the states that are cutting funding from their schools or closing companies devoted to the arts, especially theatre. It is discouraging how much theatre is sacrificed to other academic pursuits. We need to do all we can to make sure this disturbing pattern does not convince us, as a society, to eliminate or diminish the performing arts from our culture.

One person who agrees with me is Duffy Zimmerman, who wrote an article in 2017 entitled, "Why High School Musicals Should Be As Respected As Sports Programs Are." In the article, Zimmerman commented on how, in our society, we unfairly place higher importance on athletics than on the arts. While there has been a significant decrease in public school funding for theatre, specifically musicals, the opposite is true for athletics. That is a mistake which needs to be corrected. In my opinion, enthusiasm for musical productions and sports events should be treated equally when it comes to funding.

Within the article, Zimmerman pointed out that both athletes and actors audition for their roles. At these auditions whether it be for a musical or a sport, there are several people who judge the applicants. For musicals, there would be a director, choreographer, and others involved in the preparation for a performance. On the other hand, at sporting tryouts, there would be the coach, assistant coach, and others who would work with the athletes at practices. Notice how there is a similarity there.

Another comparison of musicals and sports is the amount of time and practice that goes into perfecting your craft. For both types of events, rehearsal/practice occurs multiple times a week.

Lastly, both activities require a great deal of physical and mental stamina. Whether it is attending a rehearsal for a musical or a sports practice, the participants put in a lot of time and effort. In doing so, both actors and athletes put their physical and mental endurance to the test. For both, there is a lot of physical activity, as well as strategizing and memorizing, to produce the best performance possible.

Please remember all these similarities in the future. That way, we can avoid people saying things like, "It's just a musical" or "It's just a game." Hopefully, someday we will be as enthusiastic about school theatre productions as athletic events when it comes to public school funding.

Obviously, theatre is very close to my heart. Theatre has been a part of my life for as long as I can remember, and I'm willing to defend it from the doubters. My first experience with theatre was when I was six years old. My first-grade teacher had the class reenact the story *Anansi and the Moss-Covered Rock*. This was a children's book written in 1988 by Eric Kimmel. The story is about the character Anansi, a spider, who goes around tricking her other animal friends.

The teacher cast the characters in the story from the students in the classroom. Then, as she narrated the book, my classmates and I performed it. For me, this was an extremely effective introduction to the performing arts.

A couple of years later, I performed in an adaptation of an original script called, *Egad What a Cad!*. This play, written in 1953 by Anita Bell, was tweaked a bit to make it more appropriate as a children's show. It was a huge deal for me to act in this version of *Egad What a Cad!* for a couple of reasons. First, it was the first full-length play I had ever been in. Since it was a longer play, and more of an undertaking, it took longer to rehearse.

Second, this production was done on a bigger stage than I'd been accustomed to. Previously, I had performed only in front of a small audience in a classroom. This performance was on the stage of a college auditorium. Obviously, this was a huge step-up, and a lot of pressure. Especially since I was cast as one of the male leads. Honestly, I didn't mind all the added pressure. In fact, I considered it a compliment to be given the responsibility.

Egad What a Cad! had quite an impact on my life. From that moment on, I knew theatre and the performing arts was something I wanted to be involved in.

A few years later, during my middle school and high school years, I noticed that the medication I was taking for my ADD had started to negatively affect my ability to act on stage. The intensity and duration of the "shaky hands" side effect was starting to get worse whenever I was nervous. I became exceptionally unhinged at auditions because I wanted very much to impress the directors. With my nerves on display and my shaking uncontrollable, I lost confidence, and the anxiety overwhelmed me.

Then one day, I got my big break. My high school English teacher, who was directing a show, asked me if I'd be willing to be his assistant director. I accepted without hesitation. This experience inspired me to help with other shows in high school. My love for backstage theatre didn't stop once I graduated from high school. I went on to pursue a Bachelor of Arts degree in Theatre at EIU.

While participating in theatre programs during high school and college, I earned a reputation for being one of the most reliable people working in the backstage crew. When I was in high school, the chairman of the Fine Arts Department awarded me Student of the Quarter. During the awards ceremony, he gave the following speech:

Paul shows up and the first thing he does is make sure everyone is good to go and if he could help them get there. Furthermore, Paul is someone who does not just go at a task half-heartedly. Paul asks questions and makes sure he understands what is expected of him. Paul is someone we can all depend on and learn from. (J. Hallisey, personal communication, 20007)

My reputation for hard work, dedication, and reliability continued when I was at EIU.

Days before I graduated, professors told me that I was one of the most dependable stage managers they had encountered. I can't begin to tell you what a wonderful compliment it was at the time. Having my work both recognized and appreciated is one of the greatest feelings one could ask for.

The same thing happened again more recently. I helped as assistant stage manager (ASM) for a production called *The Moors*, written in 2017 by Jen Silverman. It was performed at A Red Orchid Theatre, located in a popular area of Chicago. As ASM, I worked closely with a stage manager, Kathleen, who had obviously had years of experience. I was amazed at how professional and organized they were. While I had done a few shows and prided myself as an effective stage manager, I was only getting started compared to Kathleen. I hope one day I will be just a fraction as good as she is. I saw working with her as an opportunity to improve on my abilities, and to help make me a more effective stage manager. Therefore, I asked Kathleen many questions about the documents and software they used. Maybe too many questions for her liking, ha ha. But she just kept saying it was no problem, and they were glad to answer any questions. Their high level of patience and support was impressive.

Then, when the show ended, the most unexpected thing happened. Kathleen told me that based on my work ethic, desire to improve, and strong organizational skills, that I was going to be a phenomenal stage manager one day. I cannot begin to tell you what an honor that felt like to hear. Not only from someone who I'd worked with closely but someone who obviously saw many ASMs come and go. I guess you can say lightning struck twice as far as my hard work being recognized in the field of theatre arts.

Let's just take a moment and note how remarkable it is I was able to thrive in theatre and stage management. Research shows that generally those who have

ADD encounter limitations in organization, problem-solving, and communication. What is ironic is those three qualities are what makes a stage manager so efficient. For that very reason, I was warned by many people "Stage management may not be the best field for someone like you." They were using the stereotype to create a label about me. But I didn't allow that to stop me. Instead, I used it as motivation to show it can be done. In that regard, I was successful. This is one example of not allowing a disability to keep me down and not allowing myself to be regarded as merely "the guy with the learning disability." With help from others, and my own solid work ethic, I turned it around, and I am now seen as "the guy with a learning disability who, through persistence and dedication, has followed his dreams." That label sure sounds a lot better.

I implore everyone to find a community that accepts you for who you are. If anyone judges you, find a different group of people. The fact that theatre people do not judge is the reason why I keep coming back and why whenever I am with that community, I feel that I belong. Never have I felt that I was inferior to anyone when I was involved in the performing arts. Everyone is grateful and respectful of everyone else, no matter their role. If someone is having a rough day, they are not looked down on. Instead, they are comforted. That is what makes the theatre community so close. No one is afraid to be themselves. They are happy to be there with others like them. And in the process, to make art. I hope that you can find a group of people that can provide that feeling. There is nothing else like it.

Part Four: Tips for Overcoming a Learning Disability

I think you will enjoy the positivity in this next part of the book. As I have already discussed my failures, it is now time to talk about my triumphs. I will detail a variety of techniques I've learned to overcome my disability and to turn my challenges into successes.

Let's look at an example of how I took what was taught to me and then years later, repeated the same lesson to the next generation. When I was in middle school, I had trouble using my locker combination to open my locker. I found it extremely difficult to know when to go left and right. In addition, the numbers seemed kind of small. But then, one of the teachers at the school taught me a trick that I have never forgotten. They gave me a word association formula to help. Ready for it? Here it goes… right 3, left 2, right 1. What that means is you first go to the right and skip over the first number twice, and then land on it a third time. Then, go to the left and skip one time around, landing on it the second time. Lastly, go to the right directly to the third number. Once I memorized that process, I was able to successfully open my locker every single time.

Years later, when I was a middle school teacher, I saw some students struggling to open their lockers. It was like going back through time and seeing myself in the mirror. I taught them exactly how I learned to open my locker. Behold, they no longer had any issues opening their lockers.

This example I've provided is a perfect demonstration of what this book is about- showing the methods I've learned to fix problems so you, the reader, can use them. These strategies can work for you too. Have hope! There are ways to cope with the difficulties of having a disability.

Chapter 1: Trust People to a Point

As someone who is independent-minded and may need to work nearly two to three times harder than others due to my ADD learning disability, it is sometimes very difficult for me to ask for help. There are times when asking for assistance is a major step for me. Irrational or not, I see it as a weakness because it makes me feel like I'm not powerful enough to solve the problem myself.

This inability to sometimes ask for help made it extremely difficult in school when I was assigned group projects with other classmates. One of the first times I participated in a group project, it didn't go well. In that circumstance, my entire group dropped the ball, and everyone got a failing grade. That really had an impact on me. I couldn't stand the fact that I failed, and not only that, but I failed because of someone else's incompetence. I told myself that I would never allow that to happen again. Ever since that frustrating experience, I've wanted to be the one in charge. I felt that if I took the lead, I could ensure the entire group did well. Not only did I assume the role of group leader, but I also tried to help others correctly perform their tasks. This way, I felt confident that the job would be done correctly and efficiently.

However, by doing practically everything by myself, I sometimes did more harm than good. I didn't realize the negative impact it was having on my health. Then, one day in eighth grade, it eventually caught up to me. I was doing my homework in a study hall/resource class, which was a designated time for me to get extra help from a teacher or teacher's assistant. Alarmingly, I put my head on the desk from exhaustion, and I suddenly passed out. What I saw when I opened my eyes freaked me out. There was a paramedic checking on me while my parents looked concerned standing in the corner of the room. In another corner was the teacher, the teacher's assistant, and other students.

Needless to say, I was scared because I didn't know what was going on. The paramedics kept asking me questions to see if I remembered my name and where I was. As hard as I tried, I couldn't remember the last thing I did before I passed out. Next thing I knew, the paramedics escorted me onto a stretcher and took me to a local hospital.

While at the hospital, the doctor asked me a series of questions, such as what I remembered about my day, what a typical school day looked like, and about my diagnosed ADD learning disability. This doctor was taken aback at what I described as a normal middle-school day. I was involved in several group projects, and I was doing almost all the work myself. On top of that, I was also a member of the backstage crew for the school production of *The Sound of Music*. It was the doctor's advice that considering my ADD and all the stress I was under, I needed to make the decision to lessen my workload. Either I drop out of my commitment for backstage crew, or I let others in my group projects take on more responsibility. This wasn't an easy decision to make. Theatre had been such a crucial part of my life, and I could not see walking away from it, even for a short amount of time. Meanwhile, letting go of leading my group projects, and thereby depending on others, wasn't easy either. I thought long and hard about this. In the end, I decided to stay with the backstage crew and encouraged others in my group projects to do more without supervising them.

After that experience, I had to shift my priorities. I realized that achievements like receiving a good grade for a group assignment or being seen as a success weren't as important as my physical and mental health. By focusing so much on being successful and not allowing anyone but myself to control the outcome, I was placing unnecessary stress and pressure on myself. Once I saw the negative effect it was having on my health, I knew some changes had to be made. In a way, this was a wake-up call. I only regret that I didn't come to this realization earlier in my life.

Delegating responsibilities in a group project was one example in which I had to trust others, a skill I've struggled with throughout my life. In the past, I was disappointed time and time again by who I put my trust in. I had been a victim of lies and taken advantage of more than once. My parents stepped in and taught me how to be more selective with my trust. They often quoted an old saying that goes like this: "If you give someone an inch, they will take a mile." I took my parents' advice to heart.

To say that I've had trust issues throughout my life would be an understatement. As I grew older, I became more aware of how some people tried to take advantage of me because I suffered from ADD. Not all people, but some. I don't know why, but those with a learning disability become an obvious target for bullies and those who like to take advantage of others. It is unfortunate, but it is the sad truth and a reality we must acknowledge. People with a disability, like myself, must have their shields up and play defense when it comes to those who are out to hurt somebody. I am not suggesting that you hide your disability. On the contrary, be proud that you are different. Do not let people make you feel inferior in any way, just because you are different from them, and you may need additional support to succeed. However, realize that since you are in some ways already at a disadvantage you need to be extra careful who you trust, and be aware that some are out to take advantage.

Those with a learning disability who have encountered similar problems of trust can take comfort in the fact that you are not alone. But if I could make an important recommendation, please learn from my mistakes. Number one, find the delicate balance between guarded trust and paranoia. Paranoia can be more debilitating than a lack of trust and can deter you from your dreams. I have struggled with that distinction my whole life. I hope you can learn from my mistakes in a shorter amount of time than it took me.

Number two, I recommend practicing the skill of delegating responsibilities. This way, you can share the workload. Do not do what I did and instinctively want to be the "Big Cheese" who takes the brunt of the load in group endeavors. If you can pass along some responsibilities to others who can competently do the job too, in the end your mental health will be improved. Trust me on this!

Chapter 2: Believe in Yourself

While the last chapter illustrated the importance of trust in others, just as important is having a fundamental belief in yourself and all that you can achieve. Probably the most effective way to believe in yourself is to be passionate and to follow your goals, whatever they may be. I can be described as extremely goal oriented. When I set my mind to something, I am laser focused.

Some goals, however, take time because there are snags or obstacles that slow down the process. When that happens, it is crucial to be patient and not to doubt yourself. Rather, believe in yourself. That sense of positivity and faith in yourself will help guide you through any troubling time. I know this from personal experience. There have been many times when I had to maintain hope and find alternative ways of reaching my intended goal. It wasn't easy, but by believing in myself, I was able to adapt my plans when needed.

The first example of this form of adaptation is the way I became involved in theatre arts. As I've mentioned before, my life-long fascination with theatre started onstage as an actor, but during my middle school and high school years, I transitioned to a backstage role. My introduction to backstage theatre came when I accepted the opportunity given to me by my high school English teacher to be his assistant director. The only problem though, was that I needed to find enough time to get my homework done. Rehearsals for this show started immediately after the final school bell. By the time I got home and had dinner with my family, it was about 7:00 p.m. At that time of the day, I was exhausted, because I 'm more of a morning person. Not only that, but I knew if I stayed up too late, I would be absolutely fatigued the next day. As a solution, I woke up extremely early in the morning so I could arrive at the school when the teachers normally did. Getting to the school an hour or two before the first bell gave me enough time to complete any unfinished homework assignments. I also met with teachers, went to the library, or whatever else I needed to do. All the extra work to remain on this show was well worth it because I was happy and loved what I was doing.

Furthermore, the experience as assistant director not only allowed me to regain my passion for theatre, but it also inspired me to help with other shows at the high school, and to go on to college in pursuit of a Bachelor of Arts degree in theatre at EIU. One could conclude that from the time I agreed to help as assistant director to the time I graduated from EIU with a Bachelor of Arts in theatre was a life-defining period in my life. I would agree.

Another example of creatively altering my plans was during my five years of undergraduate school at EIU. Prior to my first day on the EIU campus, I wanted to pursue a career in education. It was something I was interested in since eighth grade, when I helped a fellow classmate with his homework during an after-school study program. I remember that time vividly. I had already finished my work early, and there was extra time before the bus came to pick up all the students. The teacher who supervised the program asked me if I could assist a fellow student with the science homework, which had come easily to me. I helped him and felt an instant satisfaction by explaining the material in a way that was understandable to him. I began thinking that I wanted to do this kind of work for the rest of my life. On that day, teaching became a passion of mine, in addition to theatre arts.

On the first day of college classes I adopted a new goal for myself- to become a theatre teacher. Once I found out it was a possibility, I jumped at the chance. I was excited at the prospect of combining my two biggest passions: theatre and education. But when the state of Illinois cut the funding for fine arts education, I needed to be certified in a second subject to teach. I was advised that English language arts would be a logical fit. Many people told me how theatre arts and language arts were interchangeable and how easy the transition would be. That wasn't the case as I struggled with my language arts classes. The most likely reason was because I'm not an avid reader, so understanding more than one interpretation of a text doesn't come as easy for me as it does for others. I realized I had to switch to a subject I was indeed good at. Since I loved studying history while growing up, I thought it would be a better fit. But after it didn't work out either, I decided to cut my losses, and drop the teaching component. In the end, I graduated with a Bachelor of Arts in theatre.

I did not, however, drop the desire to become a teacher altogether. Instead, I began my pursuit for a master's degree which would still allow me to teach. At first, I thought it could be accomplished by going for a Master of Arts in theatre at Eastern Michigan University. Yet, after one semester, I discovered it wasn't the best option moving forward. So, I transferred to Concordia University, Chicago. Since the campus was located close to where I grew up in Oak Park, Illinois, I moved back in with my family while I attended Concordia to gain a master's degree in teaching. I also worked as a substitute teacher for the local school district. Working in that job helped me gain classroom experience and aided me in determining the age level of students I wanted to teach. By the time I began to student teach, I knew I wanted to work with either third or fourth grade.

Fast-forward a few years, and I was inspired to make a career change yet again. In 2021 I had the privilege of being a long-term substitute teacher at a middle school in Berwyn, Illinois. Those unfamiliar with the term, "long term sub," it means that you are the substitute teacher for a specific teacher for an extended period of time. The assignment was for an eighth-grade co- taught, social studies teacher, and I would be working with students who had various disabilities. It was my job to ensure that they were receiving all the accommodations and academic support that was legally guaranteed to them in their IEPs. I was perfect for that assignment considering their age and my own personal experience with an ADD disability.

While working as a long-term sub, I earned a reputation of being a reliable colleague. That prompted the principal to extend my stay at the school. When the teacher who I was subbing for returned, they transferred me to another long-term position that needed to be filled. That was a huge compliment. Luckily, it was a similar position. I was the co-teacher working with special education students. There were just a couple of differences. One, the subject was science. Two, the students were in sixth grade.

I am grateful that this opportunity to work with middle school students with disabilities came about. It gave me the confidence that I could teach that grade-level. Previously, I thought it was better to stay with the younger kids. After realizing it was possible, I decided to seek an additional teaching endorsement to allow me to teach not only at the elementary and middle school level, but to teach students with learning disabilities. and other special needs as well. I will pass on my knowledge and experiences, helping them reach their academic potential, much like what was done for me when I was that age. That is why I am currently going to school at Dominican University for a Special Education Endorsement.

The moral of these stories, ladies and gentlemen, is to not to be closed-minded about new opportunities in your life. Look at how many times I've switched my major in college. It isn't because I was indecisive, but rather because I was trying to find the best career path. It took a lot of trial and error, but it was all worth it. Do not be afraid to try something new. If it doesn't work out, it wasn't meant to be. Failure is a part of life, and you must develop the ability to pick yourself up and try again. I have learned this time and time again with my ADD learning disability. I did not allow my disability to be an excuse to give up. You shouldn't either.

Believing in myself and not allowing my ADD learning disability to be a reason to simply give up comes from the fact that my family raised me to speak up for myself. However, finding a balance between persistence and pushiness is a struggle I face. There have been countless times when I've delayed doing something or contacting someone because I did not want to appear as someone who forces a decision upon another. In a way, I almost sabotage myself through this thinking. Not following up with someone as to whether they got my application/resume might have cost me a golden opportunity. Simply making the phone call, or sending the email, could make a difference. I know that now.

One example of using my initiative occurred during my last semester at Concordia University. At the time, I was student teaching a third-grade class at a public school in Northlake, Illinois. Unfortunately, I was being told conflicting reports about graduation requirements from the university administration. The confusion was due to a change that was being proposed by the state of Illinois Board of Education, called edTPA. The edTPA required that the applicant video-tape parts of an actual classroom lesson and report on it. This was being discussed as the final graduation requirement rather than taking a final standardized test. However, due to there not being a decision from the state of Illinois, this change was only in its initial discussion phase. Therefore, the dean of education at Concordia hadn't decided whether the university would update the conditions to receive a diploma. They said that because there had not been an official announcement by the state yet, they could not formally make the decision until there was some guidance on the issue in writing.

This was troublesome for me as I had not yet passed the test that the edTPA was supposedly going to be replace as a graduation requirement. Not knowing definitively what I needed to do in order to graduate created in me a sense of urgency and panic. Rather than just depend on contradictory statements, I decided to take the initiative. I contacted the state of Illinois, and they confirmed, by email, that the proposed change would indeed take effect in time for edTPA to replace the standardized test as a graduation requirement. I immediately forwarded this email to the dean of education at Concordia. The Dean, then having seen a written confirmation, made the announcement of the pending change.

Keep this story in mind when you are in a similar situation. If you're ever told differing stories, take the initiative to get the absolute facts. If it hadn't been for my family encouraging me to be assertive and stick up for myself, I wouldn't have had the courage to do what I did. The self-advocacy they taught me prevented my diagnosed ADD learning disability from dragging me down and allowed me to overcome the challenges put in front of me. Even more importantly, my ability to be assertive, when necessary, has helped me to become the person I am today, and has allowed me to believe in myself. Do the same for yourself. Believe in yourself and be assertive! No one else is going to do it for you.

Chapter 3: Challenge Yourself, Others, and the Status-Quo

A particularly important lesson that I learned throughout my life is not to be afraid to challenge yourself, others, or the status-quo. This lesson was certainly learned due to my ADD learning disability and all the struggles I had to overcome. I am somewhat used to having roadblocks put in front of me. That is why I try to inspire others not to give up, but to plow through these obstacles.

An example of challenging myself was during the transition after I graduated from Concordia University until I landed a teaching position at a private Catholic school on the South Side of Chicago. While I wanted to teach third or fourth grade, there wasn't an opening for those grades. Instead, there was a position available for a middle school math teacher and someone who could create a drama club to expand the school's fine arts program. With my Bachelor of Arts in theatre and Master of Arts in teaching, I was a good candidate for the position. After much thought, I decided to take the job. I saw it as a test of my teaching abilities because math was not my strongest subject when I was in school.

I not only challenged myself by accepting the job, but I also challenged the middle-school students by creating and implementing a whole new math curriculum. One concern communicated to me from the day I accepted the job, was that the students weren't testing well in math according to the Illinois State standardized testing system. After I examined the school math curriculum and looked through the textbooks the kids were using, I identified a huge part of the problem. The textbooks were not appropriately instructing the students at a fifth, sixth, seventh, or eighth grade level, based on the Illinois State learning standards. So, when the state of Illinois standardized tests were given, the students weren't sufficiently prepared to answer the test questions correctly. I challenged the status quo and immediately reported this to the school administration, created a revised curriculum, and ordered new textbooks.

Not only was the curriculum different for the students in my classroom, but so were the teaching methods that I used. I admit that my methods of teaching at times can be considered unconventional. This is due to the more reflective style I incorporate in the lessons and how the students learn the material. A few times I asked myself what the best approach was to teaching math. Then it hit me- emphasize memory and word association in your teaching to help the students remember, and then eventually, master the material.

I truly enjoy teaching others how to understand subjects that may have been unclear for them in the past. By learning in a new and unique way, the students are more likely to have what is referred to as a "light bulb moment." Sometimes, the class just needs a new way to approach the material and to have it explained in a way that isn't as traditional, but more relatable. This teaching style is labor intensive to be sure, but it's completely worth it when there is a connection made between teacher and student. As the pupils start to trust me, they begin to open their minds to learning, and that is my goal. Engaged students who enjoy education become eager lifelong learners.

An example of using this method was when I taught fifth graders how to multiply decimals and to indicate which product had the greater value. What made these problems tricky was one of the numbers provided had only one digit after the decimal point, while the other had two of them. For example, the students were given numbers such as 3.33 and 3.8. Since some students struggled with these problems, I taught the class to add a zero to 3.8, making it 3.80. Now, it was a number with two digits after the decimal point, yet it still represented the same value. This was a tremendous help to the students. Once they realized they could simply add a zero to the one number that had only one digit after the decimal point, making both numbers the same length, it wasn't as hard as they thought to multiply the factors.

Another time, I taught the sixth graders about the differences between acute, obtuse, and right angles. I taught them the word *obtuse* has more letters than the word *acute*. Using an unconventional word association rule, the kids could remember obtuse has more letters and is, therefore, larger than ninety degrees. They could make the same association with acute angles having less letters, and, therefore, measuring less than ninety degrees.

I knew my teaching style was successful after seeing the increase in kids' test scores. After all, numbers do not lie. The average math test scores were higher than they had been in the past. Specifically, the eighth graders scored the highest in mathematics than they had in years. I was so proud of my students, and myself. It was such a great feeling to know I was making a considerable impact on their learning.

In addition, I inspired many members of the school population to participate in the newly formed drama club. With my encouragement, those who participated in drama club successfully raised their test scores and developed a newly found appreciation for the arts. They were also able to gain an added sense of confidence by performing in front of a group of people. As an advocate for the importance of theatre, sparking an interest in these kids and increasing their confidence to perform in front of an audience made me so joyful. I felt that my positive impact was not only taking shape in the classroom but on the stage as well.

The moral of these stories is to have enough will and fight to challenge yourself and others. Do not let anyone discourage you. This is a major philosophy of mine. In my opinion, there is nothing wrong with challenging the current status quo if better results are sought.

Furthermore, do not let anyone, including yourself, stop you from pursuing a desired goal. Even if the risk results in defeat. As hard as it may be, do not allow doubt to creep in or let your self-confidence be diminished. The moment you let your guard down and the negative thoughts in, you're screwed. I learned that the hard way many times. What helped me every time was believing in myself. Believe in yourself and you will go far. If something is important to you, by all means go for it!

Take this advice, and you will thank me in the end. By challenging yourself, others, and the status quo, you will discover how strong you really are and how much of a difference you can make. Most likely, it won't happen over-night. I will not lie and say it will be easy. After all, if it were that easy, then it would not be a challenge, would it? Keep that in mind.

Chapter 4: The Dangers of Being Too Proud to Seek Help from Others

Due to my ADD diagnosis, I strongly believed that to mature, I couldn't have the answers spoon-fed to me. Instead, I needed to fend for myself and learn from my mistakes. Quite simply, I felt that if I did not learn how to pick myself back up after failing, I was doing a grave disservice to my growth and development. Additionally, when I was given feedback or criticism, I hated it if they were vague suggestions without specific details. Working in theatre, sometimes the director or those who came to see the performance would say things like, "Oh, you did a good job." There was no follow-up to that, which drove me absolutely crazy. I would then have to ask questions such as, "What was it that I did well?" I can't possibly improve on something if I am not given specifics about what I did well and what I need to do better. Since I have to work just as hard, or sometimes even harder than others, I might need some extra input on what is necessary to reach the best of my abilities.

While looking for a full-time teaching position after grad school, I came up against an unexpected obstacle. I went from interview to interview; unfortunately, I wasn't hired. I was told by potential employers how it was such a tough decision not to offer me the job. As a result, I would play mental games and replay the interview back in my mind. I tried to remember all the responses I gave, facial reactions, and such. That only led to a lot of, "What if I did this?" or "What if I did that?" scenarios. These "what if" scenarios caused me to become anxious about future interviews.

To help solve this problem, I came up with the idea of consulting a professional career coach. During these meetings, I spoke about my goals. While discussing goals was important, the career coach taught me what was arguably even more important was the skill of positive self-talk to raise my confidence and self-esteem. To give me practice with this skill, my coach had me think of life events that could help highlight my strengths. They referred to it as "selling myself and my accomplishments." So, during our mock interviews, the coach asked me questions like those I would be asked during a job interview, to give me practice on how to emphasize my strengths. By doing the exercises, I gained more confidence. The benefit of my increased confidence was proven not long after. I was able to secure a teaching position in a fourth-grade classroom at the school where my friend, Lyndsey, worked! Not only was I excited to have my friend as a colleague and to have my own classroom, but I also felt marvelous getting the job by "selling myself and my accomplishments."

While seeking help from a professional was a huge step forward, the most difficult people to ask for assistance have been my family. One would think it would be easier because I am so close to them. Yet they are the ones I have always wanted to impress the most. Therefore, there have been times when I had to balance how involved I wanted my family to be in certain personal matters.

Throughout my life, my family has helped me unconditionally, especially when it related to my ADD learning disability and all the struggles that come along with it. For example, my mom and dad were eager to consult with teachers, go to IEP meetings, and arrange for evaluations with specialists and professionals to determine what learning accommodations were necessary for me. I remember when I graduated from middle school, my standardized test results indicated I should be placed in remedial classes when I started high school. My mom was advised to call the division heads at the high school for English, history, science, and math to explain that she and my father wanted me to be placed in a general education curriculum. I am so thankful she did that. It showed her love for me and her belief in how well I could do academically with my strong work ethic and dedication.

Another way in which my mom was super helpful during my schooling was when she would edit my writing. She did not write the papers for me. Instead, she gave constructive suggestions and critiques of my work. She also provided helpful techniques on how to write more effective paragraphs and to communicate what I was trying to say. I believe if it weren't for my mom, I wouldn't be as good a writer as I am right now. And here I am, writing a book!

My father has been a great advocate as well. He is easy to talk to and communicate with, and we have a similar sense of humor, which makes our conversations enjoyable. He was able to help with assignments involving poetry and reflective thinking. Due to his love of poetry and classical literature, he helped me get in the author's mind and discover why they wrote the way they did. Expressing the right tone and purpose to make your writing understandable to your reader is a difficult skill to master. I hope I have succeeded in that from my father's teachings.

While my parents have been helpful with the academic and fine motor difficulties associated with my ADD learning disability, my older brother, Josh, helped with my social skills. When I was being bullied, he would step up and defend me. He alerted my parents if I was too afraid to tell them because I feared retaliation from the bully. If it weren't for Josh, I wouldn't have had enough bravery to fight for myself. Josh would also give suggestions about making friends. I believe these brotherly encouragements have helped me throughout my life.

Although I was able to selectively seek assistance from my family, there were times I didn't have the same courage to seek help from my good friends. While I know I can talk to them about almost anything, I have a hard time coming to them when I feel down. It goes back to wanting them to see me as someone who defies all the odds, and not someone who is vulnerable. However, through the advice of therapists and my own self-reflections, I can now admit that was the wrong choice. I should have let them see me, not only in the good times, but the bad ones as well. I am human, right? Humans have their moments of crisis.

An example of this is when I chose to leave my position teaching fourth grade in the Central Illinois area, I didn't seek help or advice from my friends. There were times when I wanted to talk to Lyndsey, who had told me about the job in the first place, or my dear friend Courtney, who lived nearby. Yet, I chose not to bother them because they had so much going on in their own lives. Lyndsey had just given birth to her second child and Courtney was working long hours. That is what I told myself as justification, right or wrong. The truth is, I had erroneously decided not to let my friends see me in a negative light. Previously in this book, I talked about how I can put myself in a "protective mode." This was no exception. I realize now it was a big mistake because I could've used the emotional support from friends who lived close by. Instead, I relied on my family who lived several hours away. I regret allowing my pride to get in my way. My desire for the label "Guy Who Overcomes All Odds" deprived me of what I really needed. I implore you not to make the same mistake. Whatever you do, don't allow an inflated sense of pride to get in the way of accepting support from the people who love you.

The moral of this story is that whatever you do, do not allow false pride to overpower your decision-making. I encountered this problem more times than I would like to admit. I did myself a disservice by allowing my desire to be self-sufficient impede my ability to ask for help. Being blinded by ego with seemingly no one to turn to, my personal health, both physical and mental, was affected. Therefore, I created more stress and pressure on myself than was necessary. Now that I can look back on the decisions I made at the time, I regret how I couldn't see what I was doing earlier. Please don't let yourself become entangled in a similar situation. Not only will you find it easier to communicate with those who have your best interests in mind, but you won't jeopardize your health with additional stress. Once you turn a blind eye to false pride, you will thank me. Your life will be so much better. Furthermore, you will be closer to your family and friends, and you will be stronger physically, mentally, and emotionally. I guarantee it.

Chapter 5: Accepting that there are Some Things You Cannot Control

Another difficultly in navigating through life with ADD was learning acceptance. You need to come to terms with the fact that some tasks are harder for you to accomplish than for others. It isn't that you can't do it, but you might need some sort of accommodation or technique to assist you. This is something I learned through all the meetings at school, all the family discussions at home, and all the support I was given along the way. Eventually, I accepted this is as a part of my life with ADD.

One life-lesson that took longer to accept was the fact that there are things beyond our control. For instance, when you make a mistake. When this happens to me, my elevated sense of paranoia kicks in. I start to have a panic attack. I assume the worst is going to happen. I can be at work and make the simplest mistake. Then, in my head, I'm overwhelmed by the fear that I'm going to be called to my boss's office.

An example of this mentality is when I was working as an assistant stage manager (ASM) for a production of *The Moors* at A Red Orchid Theatre. I had worked with Kathleen, the stage manager, for a couple of months. And then a second ASM, Lauren, was hired to help during the performances. From the moment she was hired, I had two contradictory emotions. First, I was relieved. All the work I oversaw would be less of a burden because some of the tasks could be delegated to someone else. Thereby, there was less pressure to get all my responsibilities completed. Yet, I was intimidated she would do the job better than me. After all, with my ADD mindset

I thought I must work two to three times as hard because some things didn't come naturally. That way I could be as good if not better than my counterpart. Unfortunately, for me, though, Lauren was more experienced. So, I concluded I would not perform better. In my mind, the margin for error on any task was zero.

Then, toward the end of the run of the show, a rain effect that I oversaw started to malfunction. There was some problem with the building pipes. I wanted to fix the problem but couldn't. Eventually Kathleen asked Lauren to take over. I took it personally as a reflection on my performance, an indication I was failing at my job. In addition, I felt like something was being taken away from me. All that I had left was escorting actors and actresses up a set of stairs so I could lock and unlock the door they used to do a crossover. I knew it was going to be hard this particular evening because I'd hurt my knee earlier in the day at my other job, but I wasn't going to let that be taken away too. Therefore, I did a stupid thing and kept my injury hidden. I was determined to prove how useful I was, and I wasn't going to let some minor pain get in the way of that. Consequently, I escorted the actors and actresses up the stairs ignoring the pain.

Whenever these incidents like I described occur, it is simply my mind playing tricks on me, and thereby, making me sick to my stomach. An unnecessary cycle as it turns out. The frequency in which I do this has decreased over the last couple of years. A major reason for that shift is because I've been seeing a therapist to help me with this unhealthy pattern.

My therapist and I have devoted a lot of time toward learning to accept that no matter how hard I try to be in control, there are some things I must let go of. This is hard to come to terms with for a person like me. One of the ways I learned to cope with my ADD was to have some sort of routine and control. When I am not in control, it's a bit frightening. My therapist has guided me through various talks and exercises to lead me to this form of acceptance. It didn't happen overnight though.

It took me a while to accept my limitations and have the patience to work through the challenges presented by my ADD. At first, I saw being unable to do certain things as a sign of defeat. Yet, with all the love and support I've received, as well as my own personal qualities of persistence and patience, I found a way. Please see my story as an inspiration. If I can do it, you can too.

Chapter 6: Find Your Source of Excitement and Hold On to It

I t is crucial to have joy and happiness in your life. I am sure you have heard phrases, such as, "Stop and smell the roses." Basically, I interpret that saying to mean that even when you have a lot on your plate, you need to find the time to do something that provides for a few minutes of happiness and allows you to "be in the moment." Do not let any characteristic or side effect from a diagnosed learning disability prevent you from having a sense of excitement. Through my personal experiences, I have learned that finding what excites you and then making sure it's a huge part of your life is a bit of a process. It takes a little bit of time and patience. At least it did for me.

The first step I took was to identify what I could possibly do to distract myself from everything else that was happening around me. It didn't take me long to figure it out. Theatre, of course!

Once I realized that theatre was what I needed to decrease my stress and help me peel away the labels that my ADD learning disability created, I took the second step. This was when I had the internal struggle about whether to allow other people's thoughts and opinions to define me and affect how I live my life or my ability to be my own person.

In the end, I chose to reject everything that everyone else was saying. It wasn't easy, but I found enough courage and willpower to fight through this negativity and ignore the doubters who tried to tell me theatre was not the best field for me and that it would lead to nothing but sadness and unemployment. After all, it is my decision how huge a role theatre plays in my individual pursuit of a happy and satisfying life. If theatre allows that to happen, then it will be my source of excitement. No matter what others try to tell me or how persistent they may be with their self-declared expertise.

The last and final step was to be flexible about how to have theatre in my life. I was determined to have access to theatre. If I couldn't be onstage or a part of the backstage crew, I was going to buy a ticket to see a live performance. I've had the opportunity to see some wonderful productions from the audience. One of my favorite theaters is Steppenwolf Theatre in Chicago. My parents have had a membership subscription there for many years.

Other theaters I enjoy attending because I have a membership are A Red Orchid Theatre in Chicago and the 16th Street Theater in the western suburb of Berwyn. In addition, I have the honor of being a member and fundraising chair of the Associate Board at A Red Orchid Theatre.

I have also had the opportunity to see other famous live productions at other theaters in Chicago and around the world. Some of the shows I have seen with my family and friends include *Wicked*, *Fiddler on* the *Roof*, *The Book of Mormon*, and *Hamilton*. As a young child, my family and I saw two classic Broadway productions in New York City, *The Sound of Music* and *The Lion King*. Also, while on a family vacation in Italy after my high school graduation, I saw *La Boheme* in Rome. What a memorable experience that was!

Having worked in the performing arts almost my entire life, I've gained an extreme appreciation for all that goes into it. I have earned a remarkable reputation with my peers for all the hours I have put in, and that is something I take great value in. Looking back at my life before my English teacher asked me to help him backstage and how much I struggled to be involved in theatre because of my ADD, I'm so grateful to be where I am today. I have a Bachelor of Arts in theatre, a Master of Arts in elementary education, and a long reputation as a hard-working and talented member of backstage crew.

I suggest that you search for something that brings joy into your life, much like theatre has done for me. Once you have found that "special something" hold on tight, and never let go of it. Take my advice: Do whatever you can to ensure it is not taken away. Ignore the doubters! If it is something that is important to you, fight for it!

Part Five: Conclusion

I hope you have enjoyed reading my book nearly as much as I have enjoyed writing it. I never in a million years saw myself as a writer, but it just goes to show you that anything is possible. With my diagnosis of ADD at such an early age, I had to find ways to manage the struggles and roadblocks that were in front of me. It was not easy, but I found ways to not allow the label of ADD to define me. Instead, with all the hard work I put forth, I created a different perception of myself. One in which people would see me as a man who never gives up and who achieves so much despite the many struggles put in front of him. In other words, I made my own luck.

While I give myself a lot of credit for how far I have come, I couldn't have done it without the help of others: my family, friends, teachers, and other professionals who encouraged me to succeed and to reach my greatest natural potential. Simply by knowing I had their encouragement and advocacy, I was able to find within me the fight and confidence I needed. It felt great to know so many people had my back and my best interests at heart.

While preparing this book, I found it enlightening to recall all the stories and events and their impact on my development and sense of identity. These experiences have made me the man I am today.

Now that I have accomplished my goal of writing a book about the struggles of having an ADD disability from the perspective of someone who has gone through it, it's time to sign off. I want to end on this note: Don't allow yourself to become convinced you have any less of a voice or that you are any weaker than someone who does not have a disability. On the contrary, by not giving up on a task, which takes two, three, maybe four times more effort than it does for others who do not have a disability, you are even stronger. Don't let anyone tell you any differently. Remember you are the master of your own destiny, and you are undeniably special, even if your uniqueness requires you to peel away the label others have given you.

Paul E Martin

Part Six: A Tribute to my Family

While I have referred to my family throughout this book, I would like to take some time to pay tribute to the best family one could ask for. Yes, my disability has played a major part in shaping my identity, but arguably, my loved ones have had just as much of a role. I have been blessed with a loving and caring family. My older brother, mom, and dad have done so many things for me, it would take forever to list them.

Dear Family, I'm now speaking directly to you. If I haven't made it clear through my actions or if I have not said often enough how much I appreciate your love, I hope this book helps show exactly how grateful I am. Now, the whole world will understand what I already know to be true- how great you are as individuals, and as family members. Before I go any further, I will say it once more: I love you and you are the greatest.

My mother, Iris, is one of the best moms anyone can ask for. I know everyone says that about their mom, but I mean it sincerely and with all my heart. She cares so much about people. When I would have friends over, she would indulge them like they were her own children. The moment they walked in the door, she would ask them if they needed a drink, how they were doing, and so on. That is just the type of person and mother she is. Her capacity for caring, I would venture to say, comes from her many years in the classroom as a substitute teacher. Once, I had the opportunity to go with her to work on a Take Your Child to Work Day. I saw, first-hand, how great she was with the kids and how all the children loved her. As my family says often, "She has the gift." To all the teachers around the world, I'm sure you can relate to that phrase.

My mom originally became an elementary school teacher, and later decided to pursue a career as a lawyer. She met my dad when they were both students in law school. While my dad continued to practice law for many years after law school, my mom felt she would be happier in another field. She thought of becoming a nurse, but after she realized she was too squeamish with needles, she decided to go back to teaching, which had been her original goal.

She was at almost every event of mine that I thought was important. And if she could not be there, she would feel so guilty about it. No matter how many times I tried to assure her, she still regretted not being able to make it. But let's be honest, she didn't miss much!

My mom has taught me so many life lessons. Some of the qualities that define me are in are due, in part, to how she encouraged morality and a strong work ethic. Some of my interests can also be attributed to her. She is one reason why I have such an avid interest in politics and current events, and we both share a love of theatre.

Thanks to my mom, I'm quite good at problem-solving, especially regarding crossword puzzles and Sudoku. She taught me various techniques for solving these puzzles, which I still remember. As a result, if you were to challenge me to a Sudoku-off, I would easily squash you!

Yet another quality my mother instilled in me is self-initiative. If it were not for her, I wouldn't be able to stand up for myself the way I do. I will admit I still need a little work on that, but my motives for self-advocacy were encouraged by my mom.

While all these characteristics she encouraged are admirable, probably the most identifiable quality of mine that she nurtured is my desire to help those in need. A lot of my empathy is, without a doubt, thanks to my mom. She instilled in me a great capacity for caring and authenticity.

Thank you, Mom, for everything you have done for me. I wouldn't be where I am in life without your love and constant encouragement.

What I said about my mom, and how much I love and appreciate her, can be said for my father, James, as well. I cannot express enough how great a father my dad is. While my mother had such a positive influence on me, my father deserves praise too.

My dad helped instill in me a curiosity for other languages and cultures. Thanks to my dad's love for various cultures, I'm always eager to learn about other peoples' ways of living. My father taught himself Italian and he is now fluent in the language. He came home one day after simply hearing the celebrity Studs Terkel, speak Italian on TV, and he said it sounded so beautiful that he had to learn how to speak the same way. After teaching himself Italian, he convinced me to study it in high school as part of the foreign language requirement. He spoke Italian constantly in our home and everywhere he went. He even spoke Italian to our dog! In Italian, he would tell the dog to sit and other simple commands. While that is amusing in itself, I found it hilarious that the dog understood.

My parents share a mutual love for travel. They took my brother and me on vacation to Italy multiple times. They would rent a car and we'd travel through the country. I am incredibly lucky to have enjoyed many funny and heartwarming memories from those experiences. It seems predictable that my immersion in the Italian culture, cuisine, and language inspired me to choose Florence, Italy as my destination to study abroad when I was in college.

My dad has a great love for music and literature. In fact, he is a talented musician. Although I don't play a musical instrument, he taught our next-door neighbor, Alec, how to play guitar and harmonica. My father's love for music and his vast knowledge of it is what made him such a good instructor. In fact, he briefly considered leaving the practice of law to become a teacher, but he soon found it wasn't the best profession for him. I agree with his choice because he certainly has a gift for lawyering.

I also learned the willingness to listen to everyone's perspective from him. My dad taught me the importance of considering everyone's opinion. To this day, I consider myself a people pleaser, in part, thanks to my dad. When my dad started out his career as an attorney and was considering whether to become a judge, he asked my brother and me for our insight. We offered him contrary points of view. Josh thought he should keep his current position because the salary was higher than that of a judge. Whereas I thought he should become a judge so he would have the power to tell people what to do! My father heard us both out and asked us questions about our conflicting points of view. In the end, he chose not to pursue the bench.

My work ethic is attributable to both my parents. That drive has served me well, and I have often received praise for it. My dad's admirable work ethic is evident in that he was able to become a partner at the law firm where he worked. When he retired, his name was prominently displayed as part of the firm's name on the door of the office.

Thank you, Dad, for everything you have done for me. I wouldn't be where I am in life without your love and wise encouragement.

The last family member I want to thank is my older brother, Josh. He has such a kind heart and is an awesome big brother. You're the best, Bro!

Something that Josh taught me was the ability to have a sense of humor about myself. This was a process that took many years. When I was younger, I was more serious-minded. This was in large part due to my ADD and my mindset that I needed to work hard to impress others. Therefore, when Josh tried to ease my mind and poke fun at me, I was a bit sensitive. I couldn't simply turn on and off my competitive drive like a light switch.

Then, that all changed when I was a sophomore in high school. That was when I started to become involved in theatre and interact with people who had a more sarcastic sense of humor. By hanging out with them for a couple of hours a day, five times a week, I quickly learned how to better forget all of the other things weighing on my mind and "be in the moment." Once I was more comfortable, I began to poke fun at myself. And even more, surprising, to laugh about it. Participating in theatre began the transition from being 100 percent goal-oriented, to finding a balance between being academically driven and having a sense of humor about myself. This change created the opportunity for Josh and me to better bond over the brotherly jokes he directed at me.

Like me, he has an artistic eye. We share an avid interest in films and filmmaking. In fact, he first introduced to me some of the movies that have become my favorite for many years. I'm not sure whose movie collection is larger, probably mine! Like my parents, he loves music and plays piano as a personal hobby. We both followed in our dad's footsteps and learned to speak Italian in high school.

Josh is an accomplished photographer/videographer. He graduated from DePaul University with a degree in digital cinema, which he used to his advantage by working at a specialty camera store. At the time, he not only sold high-tech cameras, but conducted in-house equipment training consultations for people who had just bought expensive cameras from him at the store. This job allowed him to utilize two of his greatest strengths: selling and knowledge of cameras.

His education at De Paul University also afforded him the opportunity and honor of working as an intern at a famous theater in Chicago, and as an on-site intern during the filming of a horror flick called *The Unborn*, directed by Christopher Nolan.

Currently, Josh is a free-lance photographer and videographer. He likes to visually direct music videos for presentation on You Tube, and he also shoots videos of special occasions, like weddings. In addition, Josh works as the media manager for a company called Metro Alive. As media manger, Josh helps to convince businesses and restaurants to join the company's client list. In return, they gain popularity via the pictures, videos, and website consultation that Metro Alive provides. This is the second job that Josh has landed in which he is able to sell and use his background in photography.

While Josh is excellent at digital cinema and will always have an artistic side, he also has a strong caring side. I believe he would make an excellent doctor or nurse. When we were all living at home together due to the COVID-19 pandemic, Josh always made sure everyone in the family ate as healthy as they could to ensure they lived a long and active life. Also, a couple months prior to when COVID-19 hit the

United States, he helped my mom after a hospital stay with a respiratory virus. He constantly reminded her to take her medication and to use her inhaler. Josh also made it part of our daily routine to check both of our parents' temperature and blood pressure. If he were to pursue a degree in the medical field, I believe he'd be very successful.

Thank you, Bro, for everything you have done for me. I would not be where I am in life without your love and heart-felt encouragement.

References

Allen, W. (Director). (2001). *The Curse of the Jade Scorpion* [Film]. Dreamwork Pictures.

Burton, T. (Director). (1982). *Batman* [Film]. Warner Brothers.

Characteristic. (2002). www.dictionary.com. Retrieved from https://www.dictionary.com/browse/characteristic.

Kimmel, E. A. (1988). *Anansi and the Moss-Covered Rock.* New York: Holiday House.

Obama, M. "First lady Michelle Obama on bullies: 'When they go low, we go high.'" PBS News Hour, July 25, 2016. [Speech audio recording]. YouTube. https://www.youtube.com/watch?v=La-q0c02aLU

Zimmerman, D. (March 2017). *Why High School Musicals Should Be As Respected As Sports Programs Are.* The Odyssey. Retrieved from https://www.theodysseyonline.com/why-musicals-should-be-as-respected-as-sports-programs

Author Bio

Paul Elliot Martin was born and raised in Oak Park, Illinois, a suburb of Chicago. Due to growing up in an inter-faith household, Paul celebrates the traditions and holidays of both the Jewish and Christian religions. With this diverse upbringing, Paul has developed a sense of global curiosity and a love of travel for Paul. While in college, he participated in a study abroad program, and lived four months in Florence, Italy for four months. He has also visited other parts of Italy, including Rome, Venice, Bologna, Milan, and the Amalfi Coast. In addition, Paul has traveled to Barcelona, Girona, Costa Brava, Prague, Berlin, Paris, Verona, and Amsterdam.

Paul has several passions that he cares about deeply. One example is the love of the Chicago Cubs. Paul enjoys watching the Cubs on TV and attending live baseball games with his friends and family at Wrigley Field. He even named his two cats Addie (Addison Street) and Wrigley (Field). I mean, if being a Chicago Cubs fan, and sticking with them for so many years despite their tendency to disappoint, then what is the meaning of loyalty?

Film and theatre are two of Paul's defining interests. He enthusiastically watches a variety of movies and has quite an extensive film collection. All his films are arranged alphabetically in his DVD towers. Walking into his home is like going to a video-store. Paul especially loves to see the films that are nominated for the Academy Awards and to predict the winners. The televised Academy Awards Night is like the Super Bowl to Paul.

Theatre also has a special place in Paul's heart. He loves to participate in and watch live theatrical productions. Ever since he was a little boy, he has been fascinated with it. He has seen productions such as Hamilton, Wicked, The Book of Mormon, West Side Story, Fiddler on The Roof, and The Sound of Music. Currently, he is a member of the Associate Board and serves as fundraising chair for the well-known A Red Orchid Theatre in Chicago.

The final noteworthy quality of Paul is his persistence. He refuses to let people define him. Growing up with attention deficit disorder (ADD), he felt as if people were trying to use that label to put him down. That motivated him even more to succeed. In other words, doubting Paul makes him even stronger and more determined. While this has been a life-long struggle for Paul, he has thrived thanks to the love and support of his family and friends, as well as the teachers and educational specialists in the local school district who devised appropriate accommodations to meet his special learning needs during his schooling years. Paul has used the services afforded to him to his advantage. He has earned a Bachelor of Arts in theatre from Eastern Illinois University, a Master of Arts in teaching from Concordia University, Chicago, and is completing an endorsement in special education from Dominican University.

Paul's ambition to help others enables him to be an effective and caring special education teacher. Growing up with the challenges of ADD, Paul loves to work with students who need someone to advocate on their behalf. And who better to inspire others to peel away the labels of their disability than someone who was in a similar situation throughout his schooling?

Made in the USA
Monee, IL
05 August 2023

40474179R00066